Jewish-German Identity in the Orientalist Literature of Else Lasker-Schüler, Friedrich Wolf, and Franz Werfel

DONNA K. HEIZER

*Jewish-German Identity
in the Orientalist Literature
of Else Lasker-Schüler,
Friedrich Wolf,
and Franz Werfel*

CAMDEN HOUSE

The cover photo is of Hugo Zitz's former cigarette factory in Dresden. Opened in 1909, it became known as the *Tabak Moschee* (Tobacco Mosque). Because his tobacco was grown in the Ynedze region in Turkey — and because Zitz was Jewish — he considered himself somewhat of an expert on Turkish and Oriental culture. His building thus reflected an Orientalist aesthetic popular among Jewish-Germans in the early twentieth century. Since 1993 the city of Dresden has been restoring it to its original splendor as a historical monument: the city plans to use the Tobacco Mosque as a cultural center. (Photo by V. Schubel, 1991.)

Lithographs by Lasker-Schüler reproduced from *Hebräische Balladen* and *Theben: Gedichte und Lithographien.*

Published by Camden House, Inc.
Drawer 2025
Columbia, SC 29202 USA

Printed on acid-free paper.
Binding materials are chosen for strength and durability.

ISBN:1–57113–025–X

Library of Congress Cataloging-in-Publication Data

Heizer, Donna K., 1962–
   Jewish-German identity in the orientalist literature of Else
Lasker-Schüler, Friedrich Wolf, and Franz Werfel / Donna K. Heizer. --
-- 1st ed.
   p.   cm. -- (Studies in German literature, linguistics, and
culture)
   Includes bibliographical references and index.
   ISBN 1–57113–025–X
   1. German literature -- Jewish authors -- History and criticism.
2. Exoticism in literature. 3. Jews – Germany -- Identity. 4. Lasker
-Schüler, Else, 1869–1945 -- Criticism and interpretation.   5. Wolf,
Friedrich, 1888–1953 -- Criticism and interpretation. 6. Werfel,
Franz, 1890–1945 -- Criticism and interpretation. I. Title.
II . Series : Studies in German literature, linguistics, and culture
(Unnumbered)
PT169.H45 1995
830.9'3256'09041-- dc20   95–43487
                                                                CIP

Contents

Preface

IN 1989 I was living in Multan, Pakistan. One day I was reading Friedrich Wolf's play *Professor Mamlock* (1933) — a drama warning Jews and communists about the Nazis' intentions toward them — when it suddenly occurred to me that, especially during the Nazi period, the Germans had characterized the Jews and the Bolsheviks as dangerous yet seductive forces coming from the East. That the Germans have had a long relationship with Asian cultures, and that the history of their attitudes toward the Orient has frequently been hostile, I was well aware; I also wondered if these historical German perspectives might not have a strong connection to German racism toward political asylum-seekers and so-called guestworkers (*Gastarbeiter*) today. In order to help me determine if the Nazis' labeling of Jews and Bolsheviks as Orientals had hit a sensitive nerve in the German public, I decided to review the history of the depiction of the Orient in German literature. When I got to the early twentieth century, I was struck by the number of texts with Orientalist themes and settings; it was time for me to investigate why this was the case. I discovered that many of the German authors who wrote Orientalist fiction in this period were Jewish and was surprised to find that no studies had been done on the phenomenon of Jewish-German literary Orientalism.

The overarching theme of this book is the construction of cultural identity for Jewish-Germans between 1900 and 1933. Using the Orientalist literature of Else Lasker-Schüler, Friedrich Wolf, and Franz Werfel, this book explores representations of Muslims and Islamicate cultures in the contexts of the history of German Orientalist literature, the more modern tradition of Jewish-German Orientalism, and the specific cultural concerns which emerged in Germany during this historically critical period. My analysis reveals how these authors — who themselves were often seen as Orientals in the German-speaking societies in which they lived — came to terms with their multiple identities as Germans and Jews by writing Orientalist literature. My book shows the diverse responses individuals in this particular social group displayed toward the exotic as a cultural construct, thereby mirroring the complexities of Jewish-German identity.

I have chosen to examine the Orientalist literature of Lasker-Schüler, Wolf, and Werfel because the similarities and differences in their personal and professional situations seem representative of other Jewish-German authors. Although German Studies today may regard all or some of them as faded stars of German cultural history, the contributions of these three authors were considered of enormous significance; it is illuminating to examine their works for notions about the Orient which influenced the German popular imagination. These authors were seen as fascinating and even heroic people by many Germans, and their works reflect the richness and complexity of their lives.

As I wrote this book it was important to keep in mind that early twentieth-century German culture is as exotic to me in some ways as contemporary Pakistani culture had seemed at first. After all, these Germans did not inhabit the same material world that I do. This book, while maintaining a theoretical methodology informed by the work of Edward Said, returns to the art of close reading. I have strived to keep the historical and biographical contexts of the authors — as best I can understand them — in the forefront of my interpretations. My hope is that this investigation will result in interdisciplinary dialogue about the larger issues concerning the politics of German identity during this era.

Although they are challenged as monolithic and static constructions throughout this book, I have elected (for aesthetic reasons) not to put quotation marks around such concepts as Orient, Oriental, West, Western, East, Eastern, exotic, etc. However, these terms are problematic and complex in their usage — both then and now — and should be understood as such. I have also capitalized the term "other" when I want to convey its meaning as "outsider," "marginalized," or even "alien." I have provided an English translation of all the German terms, titles, and quotes the first time they are referred to in this text; subsequent references, however, will be kept in the original German. All English translations of German in this book are my own.

Acknowledgments

I HAVE MANY people to thank for their support of this book. The DAAD (German Academic Exchange Service) provided a grant to pursue research in Berlin during the summer of 1991, and Kenyon College also provided financial assistance in the form of various grants. Eve Moore, Marilyn Waldman, Mark Roche, and especially Barbara Becker-Cantarino gave consistent encouragement and helpful advice through the early stages of writing the manuscript. Kamakshi Murti's generous critical readings of the manuscript in its later stages were invaluable. Profound thanks also go to Judy Sacks for the countless ways she has supported and assisted me in this endeavor, including reading and commenting on multiple drafts. Special thanks go to Marianne Rößel (Friedrich-Wolf-Archiv, Lehnitz), Maren Horn (Akademie der Künste, Friedrich-Wolf-Archiv, Berlin), Roland Knapp (Friedrich-Wolf-Gesellschaft, Neuwied), and Herr Kregelin (Stadtmuseum Dresden), whose archival assistance went far beyond the call of duty; I also thank the Friedrich-Wolf-Archiv for permission to reproduce the Wolf photograph and the same goes to the Kösel-Verlag (Munich) for the Lasker-Schüler sketches. Gerhard Huber (Freie Universität Berlin) has always helped to make my stays in Berlin go smoothly. I also acknowledge Michael Berkowitz, Ingeborg Solbrig, and Mary-Elizabeth O'Brien for sharing their research with me. My sincere gratitude for many years of confident support goes to Henry Remak and Walter Sokel, whose scholarship and teaching have been truly inspirational. I also gratefully recognize Jack Finefrock and Jan Lefevre for their important technical assistance and advice on this project. I humbly thank those women and men in Pakistan who befriended me during my stay there in 1989 and who helped me see the world and my scholarship in a wholly new way; that experience gave birth to this project. An especially heartfelt acknowledgment goes to my family for their undying and loving commitment to my academic pursuits through the years.

Most of all, I thank Vernon Schubel, who has always believed in my work and has shared with me a most extraordinary life: it is with love and the deepest appreciation that I dedicate this book to him.

1: Orientalism and Jewish-German Identity

JEWISH-GERMAN AUTHORS FACED a dilemma if they wished to write about Jewish topics between 1900 and 1933. Writing about the experience of being Jewish showed that they really were different from other Germans, possibly not truly German; yet most Jewish-Germans did not want to be seen that way. Since they were often seen as Orientals, writing about what they considered to be Oriental culture seemed to be a way out of this conundrum: while they were describing exotic Others, they could imaginatively describe themselves. Analyzing the Orientalist literature of Else Lasker-Schüler, Friedrich Wolf, and Franz Werfel, this book examines how three important authors explored and defined their identities as Germans and Jews. This investigation reveals how these Jewish-Germans constructed their identities by writing Orientalist literary works.

The term "Orientalist literature" applies to literary texts which employ Oriental themes, decoration, or settings.[1] For centuries, the German concept of the Orient focused primarily upon those regions and peoples encompassed by Western, Central, and South Asia, as well as North Africa; today it also includes East and Southeast Asia. Despite the Orient's pervasiveness in the history of German literature, German notions about the Islamicate Orient have not received much scholarly attention.[2] This investigation represents a step in the direction of filling the lacuna. It focuses on two of Lasker-Schüler's collections of short stories and poems: *Die Nächte Tino von Bagdads* (The Nights of Tino of Baghdad, 1907) and *Der Prinz von Theben* (The Prince of Thebes, 1912); Wolf's play *Mohammed: Ein Oratorium* (Muhammad: An Oratorio, 1922); and Werfel's novel *Die vierzig Tage des Musa Dagh* (*The Forty Days of Musa Dagh*, 1933). The disparate concerns of each author are mirrored in these texts, which were written in, and influenced by, distinct periods of rapid historical change; in addition, these works represent different literary genres.

These authors — who often were seen as Jewish, Oriental Others by the German-speaking societies in which they lived — wrote about Muslims and Islamicate cultures partially to come to terms with their own cultural identities.[3] Examining representations of Otherness in these works reveals the self-perceptions of the authors. The purpose of this analysis is thus twofold: first, to discern the social constructions of difference experienced within the German-speaking Jewish community in the early twentieth century; and second, to illuminate these constructs within a larger German context through an analysis of German literature's uses of Orientalism.

In order to uncover Jewish-Germans' attitudes toward their identities, I have turned to the depiction of the Orient in Jewish-German literature. Literature reflects the plurality of concerns, issues, attitudes, and opinions of a culture at a particular point; therefore reviewing Orientalist themes in Jewish-German literature provides a valid historical source for tracing Jews' cultural concerns. These depictions say less about the actual, historical Orient than about Jewish-German (and larger German) values and concerns. As Sander Gilman has pointed out, cultural stereotyping always serves to create a sense of specialness, of individuality, for societies and people. It produces a line of separation between "us" and "them": "they" are what "we" are not. Just as people's images of themselves change, so does a culture's; and the line of separation shifts with this process. What is crucial is that people believe that fundamental differences exist between cultures — even though these supposedly rigid lines change over time (Gilman, *Other* 11–13). Hence portrayals of the Orient in German literature — and its subset, Jewish-German literature — project Germans' understandings of their cultural identities (for example, their norms, values, and desires) onto what they believe Asia to represent in a given historical period. Accordingly, as I examine Jewish-German literary perceptions of the Islamicate world, I usually exclude questions about the accuracy of the information conveyed about the Orient: I am interested in exploring an aspect of Jewish-German literature and culture, not the Islamicate world. Indeed, most authors writing Orientalist fiction probably were not much concerned about the accuracy of their depictions: as artists, they did not necessarily have the same aims as Orientalist scholars who wish to present Asia realistically. One therefore only learns about German and Jewish-German culture through these Germans' depictions of what they considered to be the Oriental Other.

Until recently, little scholarship had been done on German Orientalism. In the past, much of the literary scholarship on Orientalism in German literature focused on non-Islamicate Asia. Other scholars recognized the importance of the influence of Islamicate culture on specific German authors. They tended to concentrate on uncovering the sources and evaluating the authenticity and accuracy of German Orientalist literature.[4] More recent works have directed their attention to the cultural significance of German constructions of identity and Otherness. Inspired by and reacting to the literary critic Edward Said's *Orientalism* (1978), a new generation of literary critics concentrates on the relationships between the representations of Muslim Orientals found in German literature and the cultural contexts in which the works were written. The insights in studies such as Cornelia Kleinlogel's *Exotik-Erotik: Zur Geschichte des Türkenbildes in der deutschen Literatur der frühen Neuzeit (1453–1800)* provide a useful overview of the history of German Orientalism and have influenced many of my own readings.[5] Yet only two published works specifically allude to the phenomenon of Jewish-German Orientalism.[6]

Methodologically, my analysis of Jewish-German Orientalist literature takes the insights of Said as a point of departure. In short — in his classic work on English and French Orientalism, *Orientalism* — Said contends that the West has colonized the Islamicate world in its literature, just as it did in reality. One challenge directed at Said has been about the usefulness of his arguments for German literature. The German relationship with the Orient has been unique and unlike those of either the British or the French. And though it is demanding to test Said's theories for their applicability to German Orientalist literature, it is doubly so for Jewish-German literature: while Jewish-Germans were classified as Orientals by some, others saw them primarily as Germans. Furthermore, although the Germans did not physically colonize the Orient, they did historically "colonize" Jewish-Germans by discriminating against them and, up until the end of the nineteenth century, denying them the rights and benefits enjoyed by other Germans. The methodological question I investigate is: how does Jewish-German Orientalist literature construct unique representations of Germans, Jews, and Orientals?

In order to apply a Saidian approach to German literature, one must distinguish several lines of argumentation in *Orientalism*. Said argues that, from the eighteenth century on, Europe, and in particular France and Great Britain, has laid claim to different parts of the Islamicate world. Theirs is a purely imperialist enterprise, which has succeeded to varying degrees in giving them concrete power over that region. In order to justify their position of superiority over the Islamicate world, these European powers — consciously or unconsciously — create a specific discourse which legitimizes their claims. This discourse encourages the systematic stereotyping of Muslims as Other and erects an artificial boundary between West and East, which has traditionally privileged the former over the latter: "the essence of Orientalism is the ineradicable distinction between Western superiority and Oriental inferiority" (42). The ensuing polarization mirrored in colonialist representations of the Orient results in what Abdul JanMohamed describes as a manichean allegory: a sphere of assorted yet corresponding oppositions between European and non-European, good and evil, superiority and inferiority, civilization and savagery, intelligence and emotion, rationality and sensuality, self and Other, subject and object (JanMohamed, "Economy" 82).

Said further argues that when Europeans advanced the supposed differences between the familiar (the West or "us") and the strange (the East or "them") (43), they had two goals: to justify their political and economic agendas, and to clarify their own sense of self by shaping an identity in opposition to what was deemed alien (54–55). According to Rana Kabbani, the direct and indirect results of this discourse are that Western narrations about the East emphasized especially those qualities that made Europe different from the Orient, banishing the Orient into an irredeemable state of Otherness. Two of the many themes that appear in European texts about the Orient stand out most prominently: the East is perceived as an area characterized by lascivious sensuality and inherent violence (6). Whereas the Orient is portrayed as being full of savages, both noble and ignoble, the Occident epitomizes the advantages and disadvantages of civility. More specifically, in European literature the Oriental is presented as feminine, seductive, dangerous, and backward, whereas the European is masculine, rational, progressive, and civilized (206–7). Since these constructs serve to reinforce the idea that the Orient needs to be civilized, they also justify European imperialism. As Hermann Pollig explains, another result of the use of these stereotypes is that, for many centuries, the West has seen the East with curiosity and longing on the one hand and fear and loathing on the other; it has been both attracted to and repelled by what it considers to be the splendor and horror of distant secrets (16).

Said's argument is based upon a more universal axiom (and he borrows from Michel Foucault): knowledge equals power.[7] James Clifford interprets this to mean that the person who can claim to possess expertise about a given culture is attempting, consciously or unconsciously, to exercise power over that culture, especially when that person suppresses all dialogue which might challenge their claim to expertise (258). When the West claims to have greater knowledge about the East than its inhabitants do, it succeeds in intellectually colonizing that region on yet another level. Even those European countries which did not have actual colonies in the Orient could nevertheless intellectually colonize that region in their discourse about it by creating constructions based upon the supposed differences between East and West. These constructions often serve to contrast the ahistoricity of the primitive Orient with the historicity of the educated West: the European repudiates the potential of "development, transformation, human movement — in the deepest sense of the word" of the Orient and the Oriental (208). Because it is supposedly incapable of undergoing any growth by itself, the Orient is perceived as being akin to putty, ready to be molded by the hands of European imperialists or by the minds of European scholars and authors who shape it according to their own needs and desires.

Finally, Said argues, the depiction of the Orient in Western literature is really a narrative of European constructs which are based upon projections shaped by specific European political and cultural interests. These interests as often as not coincide with a latent wish for self-reflection. Christiane Günther points out that any "dialogue" with the Other proves to be a discourse with oneself because, in order to have a discussion with the Other, one must establish a definition of self. The incongruities which appear in European representations of the Orient — for example that it is simultaneously wondrous and disgusting — point to the contradictions that Europeans experience about their own cultural identities. Visions of both the terrible and the ideal make clear that a glance at the Other always incorporates a glance at the self; that even apparently distinct representations of self and Other blend themselves imperceptibly until one cannot distinguish them (17). Ludwig Ammann claims that the relationship to one's own civilization is as complex as the relationship to the Other (42). What one really learns about when reading Orientalist literature is not the Orient, but European cultural definitions of self.

Seven years after his ground-breaking but controversial *Orientalism*, Said modified and defended his conclusions. He argued again that "the line separating Occident from Orient . . . is less a fact of nature than it is a fact of human production, which I have called *imaginative geography*" (90, emphasis added). Europeans project the status of the Other onto the Orient and view its inhabitants as merely peoples waiting (and needing) to be interpreted (93). Western scholars and authors assume they can speak for Muslim culture by virtue of the fact that they are white, non-Muslim, and European-educated (97). In this discourse, the Orient is not Europe's conversation partner, but its silent and passive listener objectified and dehistoricized by European authors. While it is stereotyped "as primitivity, as the age-old antetype of Europe, as a fecund night out of which European rationality developed, the Orient's actuality receded inexorably into a kind of paradigmatic fossilization" (94). The subtext of Orientalist literature lies not in a genuine desire to understand, and to learn from, another culture; rather, it is an assertion of power and an affirmation of its absolute authority born of the interests, claims, projects, and ambitions of European imperialism. Still, Said admits that the supposed division between West and East is neither static nor purely fabricated: cultural differences do exist, and these differences are emphasized, deemphasized, or distorted according to the historical context of European-Muslim relations (90). He wants to make scholars aware that concepts like Orient and Occident are social constructions — not manifestations of natural or divine orders. So it is equally important to scrutinize the people who are portraying the Orient as it is to scrutinize the constructions themselves.

A misunderstanding of Said's arguments has led critics to challenge the effectiveness of using his ideas to analyze German Orientalist literature. For example, Andrea Fuchs-Sumiyoshi's *Orientalismus in der deutschen Literatur* disputes Said's notions by attempting to prove that, since Germans did not actually colonize the Orient as the French and

British did, Germans did not necessarily do so in their literature. While she admits that some German authors readily appropriated the Orient for their own purposes, others like Goethe genuinely sought to learn about Oriental culture in order to bridge the gaps between East and West. Yet her interpretation of Goethe's *West-östlicher Divan* (West-East Diwan, 1819/27) to disprove Said's theses is problematic. Fuchs-Sumiyoshi assumes, for example, that Goethe pretending to have a dialogue with Hafiz is tantamount to having a real conversation. It is not: Goethe is in control of depicting both Western and Eastern cultures in his *Diwan*. He not only represents his own tradition, but also has chosen what he thinks should represent the Oriental norm. He can figuratively dress himself in Oriental garb, call himself "Hatem," and imagine he is having an Oriental experience while writing what he considers to be Oriental poetry. But the Orientals in the text are not afforded such a luxury; the Oriental is silent while the European speaks for him. Goethe's position is thus privileged; he expresses a relationship of power over the Orient, despite the empathy he may feel towards it.

Similarly, Ludwig Ammann's *Östliche Spiegel* takes Said to task. Ammann charges that Said thinks all European constructions of the Orient are not only *ipso facto* ethnocentric, but also racist. Yet Ammann does not give Said the credit he deserves for the complexities and subtleties of his arguments. Said is clearly aware of the potential hermeneutical dilemma in his position: but I do not believe Said wants to condemn all Europeans as racists when they attempt to represent the Orient, although he can be easily misread in this way. Certainly, because Said is intent upon pointing out the harm that Orientalists inflict upon Asia when they propagate "coercive" knowledge about it, he is accused of brushing aside the fact that Orientalism comes in all varieties, including "noncoercive" ones.

Said's most assailable point in *Orientalism* is his tendency to use sweeping generalizations, which often obscures the fact that, since not all Europeans are alike, their attitudes toward the Orient may differ; because Western writers have differing understandings of what constitutes their cultural identities, they may have conflicting ideas about what they perceive to be alien. Regarding Orientalism as a dialectical process thus helps the literary critic realize that Orientalist narratives represent Europeans forcing both reified identities upon supposedly alien peoples and equally reified, opposite identities upon themselves as Westerners. Hence the corollary of Orientalism is Occidentalism — essentialistic depictions of Europe by Europeans. Just as the content of the Other is dialectical, its form is fluid, contracting and expanding along with definitions of self. According to James Carrier, "since people within a society have differing interests, perspectives, and resources, they will differ in the representations they find appealing and in their ability to promulgate those representations" (197–98). In sum, there exist as many Orientalisms as there are Occidentalisms.

Depictions of the Orient in the history of German literature roughly conform to the kinds of stereotypes described by Said for this region. However, different emphases were placed upon these stereotypes at different times. For example, Cornelia Kleinlogel demonstrates that during the seventeenth century, when German literature generally devalued the body and sexuality, Turks were described as being overly lusty; in fact, German notions about Oriental "sensuality" actually revealed a great deal about German ideals of morality (3). German authors were simply ascribing to the Other that which they wanted to repress or express about themselves. Because German cultural identities changed over time, different constructions of the Orient were presented in the history of German literature. In addition, the exotic Asian Other was often perceived quite differently by members of the same community, because as individuals they had very different priorities and worldviews. Henry Remak asserts that the complex constitutions of cultures have thus demanded fluid, relative, and flexible interpretations. Hence a scholar of German literature must ask: what is exotic to whom? (54).

German literary and cultural attitudes toward the Orient have always been complicated, because they have been formulated over centuries of contact with the Islamicate world. One characteristic of German depictions of the Orient has remained constant over time: Germans see Asia as exotic. Sometimes this assessment has focused on its positive aspects (sensuality, poetry, wealth, ornateness), sometimes on its negative aspects (despotism, brutality, danger), often on both. From the Crusades to the conquests of the Ottoman Empire in Central Europe, Germans frequently entered into conflict with Muslims; the Turks, especially, have long been regarded as fascinating but dangerous neighbors to the East. Wolfgang Köhler points out that the first European academic Department of Oriental Studies was established in Vienna in the eighteenth century, not long after the Austrian Empire turned back the Ottoman invasion of its lands at the gates of Vienna ("die porta Orientis") (40). The connection between these events is clear: in order to defend themselves against future attacks from the Islamicate world, German-speaking countries would have to "know" their enemy. And yet the body of knowledge Germans have produced about the Orient is based upon hundreds of years of socially constructed representations which often have distorted the historical realities of that region of the world. Like other Europeans, Germans have often drawn a rigid line between themselves and what they see as the Oriental Other.

Because at times German society saw them as exotic Others, Jewish-German authors between 1900 and 1933 felt particularly compelled to write about the Muslim Orient — a place of even more exotic Others.

Their works display the diverse responses Germans expressed toward the Orient, even as they mirror the complex nature of Jewish-German identity. Although Jewish-Germans shared many of the cultural assumptions of the larger German-speaking community, the non-Jewish majority of German society also tended, because of anti-Semitism, to marginalize them and discriminate against them. The result was that Jewish-German Orientalist fiction — while it shares many of the perceptions expressed in other German works — nevertheless presents a unique perspective on the nature of the exotic as a system of signifying cultural identity.

The sheer number of Orientalist works by famous German authors in the early twentieth century is astounding; much of this Orientalist literature was produced by Jewish authors and in some cases even by Christian authors of Jewish heritage. Certainly many of the prominent authors were Jewish-Germans: this was the so-called era of German-Jewish symbiosis, when Jews had more power and prominence in the German-speaking world than ever before. But this fact alone does not explain the fascination for the Orient expressed in so many of Jewish-Germans' literary works. A cultural phenomenon was prompting Jewish-Germans to take an interest in the Orient and Oriental culture as never before. Their keen interest in the Orient seems to have been a response to concerns that Jewish-Germans had about their identity when three socio-historical factors were of great significance to them as a members of a minority group living in German-speaking countries. First, *all* Germans were struggling with the question of what it meant to be "German." Second, because German laws were passed which first granted citizenship (1871) and then guaranteed equal rights (1918) to Jews, Jewish-Germans had moved into the mainstream of German life, thereby fundamentally changing the way they saw themselves. Third, Jewish-Germans harbored fears about the possibilities of total German assimilation on the one hand and about being lumped together and ostracized with large immigrant communities of East European Jews on the other. This coincided with the rise of Zionism (which became a small but powerful force) and other concerted efforts to counteract the anti-Semitism that had dissipated among progressive Germans but nevertheless remained potent among conservatives.

The Orientalist works of Lasker-Schüler, Wolf, and Werfel must be seen in the context of the long tradition of German Orientalist literature, as well as in the context of the particularly complicated period of social history in which these authors found themselves. I have specifically chosen to write on the Orientalist works of these authors because they were influential writers. Lasker-Schüler was a leading figure in avant-garde artistic circles, Wolf was one of the most popular playwrights, and Werfel enjoyed a reputation as a controversial intellectual and poet. In addition, all of them were associated with German literary expressionism,[8] each had a fascination for the Orient, and all three were conscious of the fact that they were writing not only as Germans, but also as Jews. They were also acquainted with one another. Peter Jungk reveals that Lasker-Schüler admired the work of Werfel, whom she knew from the coffeehouses of Leipzig and to whom she wrote love-letters (31). Wolf, who was also a doctor, treated Werfel for his heart problems when they were in exile together in Sanary-sur-Mer, France, in 1939; the two of them also socialized with each other in France (290). Although there is no documentation of a meeting between Lasker-Schüler and Wolf, it is highly likely that their paths crossed in the literary circles of Dresden, Leipzig, and Berlin.

And yet the political, religious, and philosophical differences between these authors, despite the common points of reference between them, were significant. Because they had dissimilar ideological perspectives, attitudes toward assimilation, and ideas about spirituality, Lasker-Schüler, Wolf, and Werfel sought and found different things in the Orient.

Born in 1869 in the Wuppertal, Germany, Else Lasker-Schüler grew up to be at the center of the formation of the German expressionist literary movement, where she influenced and promoted several of the most famous avant-garde artists of the first half of the century.[9] She gave the name *Der blaue Reiter* (The Blue Rider) to Franz Marc, and this in turn became the designation for an entire expressionist art movement in Munich.[10] Because she constantly gave away her money to those she deemed more needy than herself, she lived in poverty, usually counting on friends and supporters to take collections for her at several of the biggest art happenings in Berlin. During her lifetime several important intellectuals and artists proclaimed her one of Germany's finest poets. Indeed, she received the Kleist prize (the German equivalent of a Pulitzer) in 1932 for her body of work. Forced to flee the Nazis the following year, Lasker-Schüler went first to Switzerland — where, despite the fact that she was in an officially neutral country, she was beaten on several occasions because she was Jewish — and then to Palestine. She died there alone, still in exile, in 1945. Until the end of her life she remained outspoken, eccentric, and true to her ideals: one of her final projects was to convince Jews and Arabs to build an amusement park in Palestine, so they could learn to have fun together and enjoy each other's company.

Friedrich Wolf became what many people today would consider a renaissance man.[11] He was born in 1888 in Neuwied, Germany, on the Rhine River. In 1903, at the beginning of his adult life, he joined the *Wandervögel*, a back-to-nature youth movement, whose ideals were both romantic and *völkisch* (nationalistic). In 1908 he went to the University of Tübingen to study medicine (with a specialization in psychiatry). There, because of his natural, rugged good looks, he was asked by the university to pose in the nude for a statue of an athlete, which was erected on campus and remains there today. During World War I he served as a doctor on the front, was wounded twice, and began writing expressionist, antiwar poetry. After finally having himself declared a conscientious objector in 1918, he was sent to Dresden to continue serving as a doctor until the end of the war. After the war, he began practicing homeopathic medicine, became an advocate of vegetarianism, and wrote one of the most significant medical books of the Weimar period: *Die Natur als Arzt und Helfer* (Nature as Doctor and Friend, 1928). He also became a communist, organizing workers, providing free medical services to the poor, and writing plays designed to inspire the masses to seek various kinds of liberation. Among his many popular plays, *Cyankali* (1929) became the first pro-abortion, free-choice drama ever staged, and *Professor Mamlock* (1933) was one of the first plays to warn Jews and communists to flee Germany. One of the first intellectuals driven out of Germany by the Nazis, he fled to France, but was later interned there in the concentration camp in Le Vernet. He managed to escape, and spent the rest of his exile in Moscow. He returned to the newly-formed German Democratic Republic after the war, where he lived in a house built under the Nazis by slave labor from the nearby concentration camp Sachsenhausen (Oranienburg): he never wanted to forget all those who had suffered and died under German fascism, including his fellow Jews. He died in this house in 1953. Today, unfortunately, he is perhaps best known as the father of two of East Germany's most (in)famous sons: the socialist-realist film director Konrad, and head of the secret police Markus.

Franz Werfel became known as an important expressionist poet early in his career.[12] Born in 1890, he grew up in Prague, his birthplace. There he later socialized with members of the prominent Zionist group Bar Kochba, which included Martin Buber and other famous intellectuals and artists. He was drafted and served as a soldier in World War I, but was released for medical reasons in 1915. He moved to Vienna in 1917 and became well-connected in artistic circles, thanks in part to his love affair with the socialite Alma Mahler, whom he finally married in 1927. He began his literary life as a composer of socially critical pacifist poetry; later he became principally a novelist. As time went by, Werfel grew more conservative in his views. After fleeing the Austrian Nazis, Werfel became one of most successful German emigrés in America; some of his works — such as the *Song of Bernadette* — were translated and filmed in Hollywood. He also became a controversial theologian whose notions about Jewish-Christianity are still studied in departments of religion today. Although he was a great admirer of Catholicism, he nevertheless refused to convert. He died in exile, surrounded by friends and family in California.

Despite their fame as German authors, these artists were still regarded, to varying degrees, as outsiders by the public. They were seen not only as Jews but also as Orientals by segments of the German public. For example, in 1917 the literary critic Kasimir Edschmid — as quoted in Paul Raabe — used Orientalist notions to compare Lasker-Schüler and Werfel as artists. He believed that all of Asia had been rendered lyrical in Lasker-Schüler's strange, poetic vision, whereas Werfel was a prophet from the East who represented a European ethos (105–6). An article in the Nazi *Völkischer Beobachter* from 1931 also refers to Wolf as an Oriental, proclaiming him one of the most dangerous representatives of Eastern Jewish bolshevism, despite the fact that he was a Westerner.[13]

I have chosen to use the blanket term "Jewish-German" to designate those Germans ethnically and culturally associated with the Jewish faith community. Most non-Jewish Germans regarded Jews as a fairly undifferentiated minority group; as the cultural critic Sander Gilman explains it, for Europeans throughout history a Jew has been simply a person regarded and treated as a Jew (Gilman, *Self* 11). Among Jewish-Germans, however, questions of identity were more complex. Issues surrounding one's ethnic (German, Yiddish, or Hebrew-speaking), religious (secular, practicing, pious) and cultural (Western or Eastern) identity were important. Because, especially during the period from 1900 to 1933, Jewish-Germans had different ideas about what being a Jew meant, I have tried to let the authors I examine define what they mean by this by looking at their literature. For this reason, I have opted to use the term Jewish-German instead of the more conventional term "German Jew," which presupposes that they thought of themselves first and foremost as Jews, rather than as Germans. Certainly this issue remained unresolved in the cases of the three authors examined here, although the evidence seems to suggest that they considered themselves to be as thoroughly German as Jewish. Furthermore, I have elected not to distinguish between German-speaking peoples from different geographical regions. In this study I refer to all speakers of German as "Germans" because German-speaking peoples usually believed they shared a broadly defined, common, cultural identity — especially since the German-speaking regions of Central Europe were fluid during this period.[14]

The years 1900 to 1933 were, in many ways, critical for the formation of Jewish-German identity.[15] The period was characterized by flux on many levels: politically, socially, economically, and culturally. One need only look at some of the major historical events taking place in Central Europe at this time to get a panorama of this era of rapid change: the intense expansion of industrialization accompanied by its many socio-economic effects, the demise of empires and the formation of new nation-states, economic booms and busts, significant technological breakthroughs, experimentation with new forms of living and criticisms thereof, and the horrors of the First World War and its aftershocks.[16] German-speakers responded to these changes in many ways, including by requestioning what it meant to be German, just as they had done in previous periods of historical upheaval. Intellectuals, especially, were engaged in pondering various aspects of "the German question." Many of the German literary and artistic works produced thus mirrored the sense of insecurity about ethnic or national identity which was part of the cultural milieu at that time. For example, the plays of Hugo von Hofmannsthal, the novels of the Mann brothers, the stories of Robert Musil, and the paintings of George Grosz all expose these concerns.

Their questions about cultural identity seem well-founded: in a relatively short period the newly-formed, German-speaking nations had emerged out of relative insignificance to become leading players on the world stage, in one capacity or another. They had become quintes-sentially modern and bourgeois, formidable economic and military forces, and colonizers of sections of Africa and Asia. But what was their specifically German contribution to the world? The concept of Germans being a "*Volk*" provided an answer to their question. According to the historian George Mosse, the search for a "German soul" in the early twentieth century resulted in a reencounter with "myths like those about the Germanic gods or the equally ancient Edda — myths which pointed to man's substance and gave him roots" (Mosse, *Beyond* 47). In fact, this movement grew out of the philosophies of the late eighteenth and early nineteenth centuries, and continued through the twentieth century. *Völkisch* thought was a product of a revolt against modern, industrial capitalism and its accompanying alienation; a quest for a unique, transcendent, yet organic, genuine German character ("soul") which bound together all German-speakers and gave them a common (and even national) identity. This *völkisch* ideology had mass appeal because it emphasized a stable, unchanging, absolute German identity in the face of changing and uncertain times. Its attractiveness to the middle class grew out of its promise to focus on spiritual and fundamental values while seemingly avoiding crass politics. It also appealed to youth, providing an alternative to politics as usual, by revolting against bourgeois materialism. Instead it favored a return to neoromantic values that appeared to counteract the alienation felt by humans living in a modern society: spiritual fulfillment, closeness to nature, a sense of meaningful community, etc. Certainly, not everyone joined *völkisch* movements or groups; yet *völkisch* ideology had a significant impact on German culture from the nineteenth century onwards. It even affected those who rejected it or were denounced by it — including many leftist intellectuals, Jews, and others whom this ideology deemed to be outsiders.[17]

Since, however, the very notion of national uniqueness meant self-segregation from the foreign, *völkisch* ideology was one of exclusion. Mosse notes that, more often than not, Jews were the ones branded as outsiders (*Germans* 14). The rise of German nationalism — the search for "authentic" Germanness — was usually accompanied by anti-Semitism, because Jews were deemed so different that it was thought impossible for them to be Germans: they purportedly lacked the spiritual foundations of the *Volk* (60). Over time, this position was modified somewhat by Germans who argued that some Jews could be assimilated into mainstream German society. Some *völkisch* thinkers thought a small segment of the Jewish population could be capable of "transcending" their Jewishness; still, they proceeded with caution with even these Jews, because their Jewishness was seen as innately hostile to all that the German *Volk* represented. Germans, they claimed, were inherently nonmaterialistic, close to the soil, healthy, and virtuous whereas Jews were materialistic, urban and cosmopolitan, corrupting, and evil. Yet they did not believe that the condition of the individual Jew was hopeless. Assimilation was only possible for a few; most Jews would remain untrustworthy, antagonistic foreigners living in the German fatherland (19). Even during the Weimar Republic, explains Ruth Gay, when most Jewish-Germans considered themselves to be fully assimilated into German society, *völkisch* anti-Semites charged that a Jewish love of German culture was merely a mask designed to hide their alien nature (186).

The identity issues with which Jews were struggling in the nineteenth and twentieth centuries mirrored those of Germans in general: how much did they want to stand out as a unique culture, and how much did they want to resemble others? At various times in history Jewish-Germans had been regarded by the larger, German-speaking population alternately as Germans or as non-Germans. Especially starting in the eighteenth century — when Jews first moved out of the ghettos — Jews and Gentiles alike debated the advantages and disadvantages of Jewish assimilation, acculturation, and separatism. During the period from 1900 to 1933 Jewish-Germans were assimilated into mainstream German life more than ever before. Most lived comfortable, bourgeois lives; they were integrated into German society during the Wilhelminian years, suffered no official discrimination during the Weimar Republic, and achieved a high level of prominence because a disproportionately large number of Jewish artists and intellectuals were highly visible as shapers of German culture. Mosse explains that they had been rejecting their Jewish cultural traditions and adopting non-Jewish-German culture for so many years that they habitually identified themselves as being German instead of Jewish (*Germans* 113). Appropriately, asserts Frederic Grunfeld, because Jews by no means constituted a homogeneous group with a shared set of objectives, they were more often clearer about what it meant to be German than what it meant to be Jewish (8). Most Jews felt themselves to be German first and foremost; they expressed this in their dress, language, cultural preferences, and patriotism. Ruth Gay posits that secularism ordered their lives more than affiliation with a particular synagogue, but those who still practiced Judaism tended to belong to either Conservative or Liberal sects — some of whose services were held in German and had adopted liturgical or stylistic elements from Christian churches — rather than Orthodox or Reformed sects (155–59).[18] By 1916, fully one-half of the Jewish-German population (270,000) belonged to the *Centralverein deutscher Staatsbürger jüdischen Glaubens* (Central Union of German citizens of the Jewish faith), which fought against anti-Semitism while remaining so patriotic that it was jokingly dubbed "the central union of Jewish citizens of the German faith" (206–7). The desire for total assimilation was so strong that many Jewish-Germans participated in *völkisch* movements, particularly those oriented toward youth, as they wanted very much to be seen as part of the German *Volk*: they rejected the cosmopolitan modernism usually associated with Jews in favor of the mythical, romantic notion of relating to the German fatherland. Most Jews felt themselves to be so integrated, so solidly German, that by 1930 one-fourth of all Jews were married to non-Jews (254).

Yet in the background non-Jewish German racism still lurked: no matter how tolerated or even accepted Jewish-Germans became as Germans in the generic sense, anti-Semitism — in both subtle and glaring forms — still played a role in daily life. Class often determined how much discrimination Jews suffered; generally, the more upper-class one was, the less one suffered. While the dream of coexistence between Jewish and non-Jewish Germans became a reality in principle, explains Marion Kaplan, in smaller-scale everyday interactions Jews were not always fully accepted as Germans (ix). During this period of German-Jewish symbiosis, claims Grunfeld, anti-Semitism did not cease to exist, but usually presented itself as an irritation; a not so minor manifestation of it materialized as Gentile Germans grew increasingly resentful of the successes Jews had achieved under integration (19).

Contributing to the problem of anti-Semitism was the fact that Germans often saw Jews as being culturally more Oriental than European: since their roots were perceived to be in the East (Eastern Europe or even ancient Israel/Palestine), Jews were regarded as Orientals. Non-Jewish Germans used the designation Oriental pejoratively to highlight differences between the Jewish and Gentile German cultures and religions. As Mosse notes, the nineteenth-century author Karl Emil Franzos proclaimed that, whereas Germans were fully European, Jews were half-Asiatic (*Germans* 46).[19] And yet, Grunfeld observes that by the first part of the twentieth century, most Jewish-Germans had only a vague sense of coming from the East (7). They saw themselves as bearers of the Western ideals of liberalism, enlightenment, and high culture. Many assimilated Jews looked down on those Jews — especially *Ostjuden* (East European Jews) — whom they perceived to be traditionalistic, backward, and primitive: in sum, Oriental. Pogroms in Russia at the turn of the century had driven half a million Jews westward, into Central and Western Europe; many of these decided to make German countries their new home because of the relatively liberal laws and high standard of living. These Eastern Jews represented all that the assimilated German Jews thought they had left behind them in the ghettos of the eighteenth century: a "lack of space, filth, milling crowds, the accents of an unpleasing language," in Goethe's words (Mosse, *Germans* 46). Ruth Gay asserts that their presence embodied a sore reminder of the past and a potential threat to the aspirations of Jewish-Germans to no longer be perceived as anything other than fully German (230).

Meanwhile, other Jewish-Germans feared the potentially negative consequences of total assimilation. The possibility of the disappearance of Jewishness and a perceived lack of cautiousness on the part of integrated Jews contributed to the formation and rise of Zionist and separatist movements. Since the Enlightenment, Jews had labored to be accepted as "civilized" (that is, Western) because of their long history as being seen as "uncivilized" (or Eastern) by the rest of Europe.[20] This need to be seen as civilized often led Jewish-Germans to unquestioningly adopt the "high standards" of German culture, including those which oppressed them. In this context, claims Mosse, those who tried to completely assimilate into mainstream German society deemed themselves "good Jews," while those who rejected total assimilation were deemed "bad Jews" (*Germans* 71).

Although most Jewish-Germans seemed to accept this resolution, Ruth Gay notes, some felt it was time to reexamine the truths of Jewish identity and faith (244). Those Jews who turned toward Zionism comprised a tiny minority. At the height of its popularity in 1920, only one-tenth of the total Jewish population in Germany — including both German and East European Jews — proclaimed themselves Zionists. Although they were a small group, they influenced many Jewish-Germans in one way or another. Primarily attracting young and wealthy Jewish-Germans as members, as well as *Ostjuden* who had been excluded from mainstream Jewish-German groups, Zionism advanced not just a political agenda but also a means of raising the much-battered Jewish self-esteem (209). It is not incidental that Zionism came into being in an age when Germans were developing their sense of nationalism and *völkisch*ness; George Mosse argues that Zionism represents a form of Jewish *völkisch*ness. He has convincingly documented the similarities of German and Jewish *völkisch* ideologies: both express a longing for a sense of specialness and cohesive community (Mosse, *Germans* 88–89). Martin Buber, one of Zionism's founders and most eloquent spokespersons, transformed the ideals of *völkisch*ness with the idea of ending European Jewry's sense of alienation. Modern Jews had become uprooted from their traditions, religious, and cultural heritage, he argued. There was no further need for anxiety on the part of European Jews about who they are and how they fit into the greater scheme of things, explains Donald Niewyk: Zionism provided a mystical route back to their Motherland, the Orient, where their roots lay and their identities were secure (145).[21] The Jewish cultural critic Ella Shohat confirms that this notion arose logically:

> the particular European Jewish historical experience [is] that of a dispersed, cosmopolitan, and syncretic people with an ambivalent relation to the very idea of the East. On the one hand, Jews of the diaspora have been inextricably mingled with the life of the West, yet Jews are also linked to the East. As an *ethnos* with historical roots in Palestine, speaking a Semitic language, whose religious idiom is intimately linked with the topography of the Middle East, European Jews are connected by tradition to the East, and have often been seen as an alien "Eastern" people within the West. (123)

The Zionist vision of Buber and others included finding a way for Jewish-Germans to adopt aspects of the German majority culture while maintaining a separate religious identity and sense of roots. Jewish-Germans could live in two worlds at once — those of the Occident and Orient — and feel good about it.

Westjüdische (Western European Jewish) German Zionists argued the need to unite with their *ostjüdischen* (Eastern European Jewish) brothers and sisters. The Eastern Jews were romanticized by Zionism as the conservators of the Jewish traditions and values the Western Jews had lost; as such they were in possession of a superior spiritual power. Ruth Gay points out that Western Jews depicted themselves as having the superior education and know-how to make an actual return to *Eretz Israel* possible (234–35). Mosse comments that these ideals particularly appealed to the Jewish youth who saw in this movement a rejection of negative stereotypes of Jews as well as a rejection of their liberal Jewish parents, whom they believed were overly urbanized, materialistic, intellectual, and alienated — in sum, bourgeois. Their earlier involvement with German *völkisch* movements of various sorts prepared them for joining Jewish ones. The focus on the importance of a closeness to nature and a spiritual connection to and love for the homeland — underscored by both these movements — was easily transferred from Germany to Palestine (*Germans* 95).

In this way Zionism both typified and departed from the imperialist ideology then prevalent in Europe as it concerned the colonizing of the Orient. Shohat argues that, on the one hand, the tenets of Zionism reveal the Jews' connection to the social conditions of Central Europe from the beginning of the nineteenth to the twentieth centuries: Zionism reacts against anti-Semitism but also acknowledges the swift development of capitalism and its accompanying imperialism. Zionist ideas about Israel are certainly linked to Western colonial ideologies, using colonialist-influenced language and promoting imperialist designs on the Palestinian land and people. The colonialist mentality which regarded non-European places as "lands without people" cannot be separated here from the Zionist concept of a Jewish people in need of land. On the other hand, Shohat insists, Zionism should not be simply equated with colonialism or imperialism. Unlike other forms of European imperialism, Zionism responded to a thousand years of oppression and, furthermore, metropolis and colony in this paradigm were located in the same place. Indeed, Israel has always functioned as the symbolic locus of Jewish classical identity. The Zionist ideal of Israel, therefore, does not merely constitute a classical case of European colonialism, since "the notion of a return to the Motherland (a view of the land as belonging to the Jews, with the Palestinians as mere 'guests'), departs from the goals of traditional Western imperialism" (Shohat 124–25).

In the long run this Jewish-German attempt to find synthesis in *völkisch*ness failed, because it paradoxically forced people to choose between being seen primarily as either Jewish or German. Sadly, it also played into the hands of anti-Semites who were all too eager to prove that Jews could never be Germans. They manipulated Zionist propaganda to declare that Jewish blood does indeed point toward the Orient, that Jews wanted to return to Palestine because they knew they did not belong in Germany. The sense of security which Zionism hoped to provide Jewish-Germans was undermined in the hands of *völkisch* anti-Semites, whose numbers were steadily increasing by the 1930s. Assimilated Jewish-Germans' dreams of total integration and the Zionists' dreams of fostering pride in a sense of uniqueness had become nightmares: their hopes and desires were quashed when the Germans gave the Nazis power.

2: Imagining the Orient

IN THE MIDDLE AGES the first extensive German contact with the Islamicate world came through the Crusades. German interests, explains Andrea Fuchs-Sumiyoshi, lay in protecting Christianity from the growing influence of Islam and in preserving the Christian world order in Europe (19). Muhammad, the revealer of the Qur'an, was an important figure in the literature of this period.[1] From the Crusades up until the Enlightenment, Germans represented Muhammad in an almost universally negative way. German literature usually described him as a "false prophet," a great *Betrüger* (deceiver), an anti-Christ (Fuchs-Sumiyoshi 13–14). The reasons for this perception were twofold: first, Muhammad — proclaiming himself to be God's latest prophet — was considered a threat to Christian doctrine. Second, the establishment of powerful and successful Islamicate empires was a potential threat to the Christian political and social order of Europe. Therefore, literary works from this period, such as the epics *König Rother* (King Rother, 1200) and Pfaffe Konrad's *Rolandslied* (Song of Roland, 1180), tended to encourage a German religious polemic against what it understood to be the capriciousness and despotic gruesomeness of the Islamicate Orient.

European contact with the Orient also produced another, more positive reaction: it evoked in Europeans a fascination for the marvels of the highly developed Islamicate world, many of the technological and artistic achievements of which had not yet developed in Europe. Texts like Konrad Fleck's *Flore und Blancheflur* (Flore and Blancheflur, 1220) described the wonders of the Orient, accentuating at the same time its decadence. And the epic *Herzog Ernst* (Duke Ernst, 1170) goes so far as to claim that the Orient is such a fantastic place that it contains an entirely different, more amazing species of humans than in Europe. Yet, even in these depictions, the authors still imagine the Orient as a potentially dangerous place, where they need to guard against being enchanted and deceived by its magnificence: the theme "all that glitters is not gold" underlies many of these epics.

With the Ottoman invasions of Europe (1453–1683), the image of the Oriental — and especially the Turk — grew decidedly more one-sided. Pollig claims that European fears toward the Turks set the tone in German Orientalist literature (18). Andreas Gryphius's *Catharina von Georgien* (Catharine of Georgia, 1657) represents negative German attitudes toward Islamicate culture during this period. It tells the story of a kidnapped European queen who martyrs herself for the honor of her

Christian faith and country rather than submit to the sexual advances of a Persian ruler. Her character traits contrast sharply with those of her Muslim admirer: whereas she is constant, virtuous, and spiritual, he is fickle, cruel, and worldly. In his drama Gryphius plays upon German fears of a Turkish (and Muslim) invasion to construct a Muslim character who serves as a foil to the Christian values the author wishes to instill in his public. His message is that Germans should be like Catharine, who is a good Christian rewarded in heaven for her faith; those who lead worldly, decadent lives based upon the vanities of life are as bad as Orientals. Germans used images of Oriental sensuality as a counterpoint to the values of chastity and purity espoused by Europe's churches; hence, asserts Cornelia Kleinlogel, the depiction of the "lustful Turks" arose from projections of those sexual desires repressed by the churches in Germany (10).

By the time Central Europeans drove the Ottomans out of the region at the turn of the eighteenth century, the Enlightenment and its values had begun to take hold in Germany. Both these events had a positive effect on the German attitude toward Muslims, Islam, and Muhammad. Fuchs-Sumiyoshi explains that, because the Turks were no longer present in Central Europe, they, their religion, and their religion's founder were no longer considered as threatening by many German intellectuals (27). At the same time, Enlightenment values of religious tolerance — combined with critiques of Christianity — and a humanist search for universal human ideals cleared the way for a more positive reception of the Orient, notes Pollig (19–20). The introduction of the *1001 Nights* to European culture had the positive outcome of reasserting the view of the Orient as a romantic and wondrous place.[2] Furthermore, contact with and interest in the region increased dramatically as Germans began to travel to the Orient while other Europeans colonized it.

These developments had the effect of considerably changing the tone of German Orientalist literature. For example, in his poem "Mahomets Gesang" (Song of Muhammad, 1774), Goethe sings the praises of Muhammad, whom he describes as a vital young *Genie* (genius) who matures into a powerful figure and changes world history; but it is his universal greatness — and not his teachings — which Goethe underscores. According to Ingeborg Solbrig, Goethe used the figure of Muhammad to promote the values of the German Storm and Stress literary movement ("Rezeption" 112). Likewise, in his *Ideen zur Philosophie der Geschichte der Menschheit* (Ideas on the Philosophy of the History of Humanity, 1776), Herder claims that, because the birth of humanity took place in the Orient, it deserves greater respect and consideration. He argues that Western study of Eastern culture could lead to greater understanding between all peoples and a rejuvenation of the West. Lessing's drama *Nathan der Weise* (Nathan the Wise, 1779) promotes the idea that Islam, Christianity, and Judaism are unique, but equally valid and related religions. He thereby champions the ideals of tolerance and respect between Western and Eastern peoples. Mozart's opera, *Die Entführung aus dem Serail* (The Escape from the Seraglio, 1782), presents a new version of the old European trope of Western women kidnapped by lustful Muslim rulers: Mozart depicts the ruler as humane and enlightened, as opposed to his assistant and foil, who is a stereotypically corrupt Turk. The opera conveys the message that even supposedly debauched cultures can produce honorable people.

In sum, during the eighteenth century many German writers depicted the Orient positively as a means to critique their own societies by presenting alternative ideals (especially those of the Enlightenment), which they made especially attractive with exotic trappings. This is not to say that, from the 1700s on, depictions of the Orient were all positive. In fact, the long and contentious history of Europe's relationship with Muslims and the contrast of this with its new-found fascination for the "wonders" of the Orient — the simultaneous existence of disapproval and affection for the East — characterizes the contradictory attitude of German writers toward the Orient which, Ammann points out, would prove decisive for the entire further development of German Orientalist literature (15).

By the end of the eighteenth and the beginning of the nineteenth centuries, a Romantic view of the Orient had begun to take shape. Friedrich Schlegel's influence on this image of the Orient was significant. In *Geschichten der alten und neuen Literatur* (Histories of Old and New Literature, 1815) he propounds the notion that the Orient is a timeless, geographically boundless place of spiritual and creative renewal.[3] Like Herder, he believes Germans need to harken back to the Orient to rejuvenate their decadent culture. For Herder, notes Fuchs-Sumiyoshi, Oriental poetry represents the highest form of the Romantic because of its mystical and mythical qualities (54). Novalis's *Heinrich von Ofterdingen* (Henry of Ofterdingen, 1802) supports this notion. In it a young German man (Heinrich) "learns" from an Arab woman (Zulima) that the Orient is magical and wondrous. Thus Oriental poetry epitomizes the highest ideals of Romanticism: mystical and mythical experience.[4] And in the *West-östlicher Divan* (West-East Divan, 1819/27), Goethe assumes the persona of Hatem and mimics Oriental poetry. He does so due to his appreciation of Persian poetry, and because he wishes to synthesize the best of the Eastern and Western poetic traditions to revitalize European literature.

Yet for the Romantics the Orient remained simply a source of inspiration and a projection of longing. As Henry Remak explains, for the Romantics exoticism was not only the exploration of a strangely foreign culture, it was a state of mind (56). After all, what enchanted and bewitched the Romantics was what they perceived to be the exoticism of the Orient, not the historical realities of the region. As much as the Romantics advocated the exploration of different national, ethnic, or cultural identities, their exoticism arose from and served other primary purposes. It provided diversely blended geographic and cultural backgrounds that served as outlets for Romantic frustrations and nostalgia, and provided alternative options to what they experienced at home (62). Like other German writers before them, the Romantics projected onto the Orient what they wanted to see.[5]

Given that many early twentieth century artists looked back to the Romantics for inspiration, it is not surprising that many German-speaking authors wrote Orientalist literature. Partially because of recent archeological discoveries, ancient and modern Egypt had become the subject of many German novels, plays, and poems in the nineteenth century.[6] According to Fuchs-Sumiyoshi, Friedrich Rückert's free translations of Persian poetry made that genre more accessible to the German public (108). In addition, literary and artistic movements throughout Europe around 1900 — for example, fauvism in France, Jugendstil in Vienna, and expressionism in Germany — used Orientalism to explore new ideas about art and society in a mythical Eastern setting.[7] The artists in these movements sought non-Western inspiration in hopes of finding new possibilities for expression in a society which they felt had become increasingly culturally oppressive. Christiane Günther explains:

> Um 1900 griff solch eine tiefgreifende Unruhe um sich. Aus einer Periode scheinbar stabiler Sicherheit heraus wandten sich Dichter vor 1914 an die außereuropäische Fremde, um von dieser Lösungen für individuelle und überindividuelle, europagewachsene Probleme zu finden und sich an der kulturellen Fremde neu zu definieren. Diese Dichter fühlten die unterschwellig sich anbahnende geistige und reale Katastrophe der europäischen Zivilisation; ihre Unruhe, die unter dem Begriff "Kulturkrise der Jahrhundertwende" in die Literaturgeschichte einging, ist auch durch diese Vorahnungen zu begründen. (286)

> (A deep sense of restlessness had gained ground around 1900. In a period of relative stability, authors before 1914 turned toward the non-European Other in order to find solutions for European individual and social problems and to redefine themselves in new ways. These authors sensed the subliminal, self-created intellectual and real catastrophe of European civilization; their uneasiness, labeled the "cultural crisis of the fin-de-siècle" by literary history, is further accounted for by these presentiments.)

Artistic movements accordingly experimented with styles and decorations they considered to be Oriental. The artists in these movements constituted a larger tradition in European literature which had adopted an Oriental voice in order to revitalize Western literature, which they saw as ineffective due to its clichéd use of language.[8] European artists characterized the so-called Eastern style as containing flowery, poetic language, esoteric, mysterious references, and mystical motifs — all of which contributed to the idea that Oriental literature provided a nonrational and emotional counterpoint to a rational, Western tradition characterized by unimaginative language.

Many artists also experienced the Orient for themselves through Europe's colonization of the region, which intensified in the nineteenth century. As Germany became a minor colonial power in Africa and China and enjoyed rapid technological and industrial development at home, German writers around the turn of the century began to express a growing identity crisis. German authors deliberated about the colonized Orient in conjunction with their situation at home and expressed their perceptions in literature. From the symbolist to the expressionist movements, German authors experimented with foreign settings, styles, and philosophies, signaling their attempt to escape from their unsatisfactory lives and to search for different ones (Günther 12).

One of the goals of Orientalist German literature in this period was to understand the cultural Other in order to propose alternatives to events at home. In the context of other contemporary, escapist movements, Orientalism proved to be a new, original form of European criticism in which the foreign culture provided the opportunity for people to reconsider potential alternatives to the ideals and socio-political assumptions of their own culture. Günther posits that Asia became the stage for a European debate about its cultural identity, its missed opportunities, and about its future opportunities to adopt Asian alternatives or to reject them (284–85).

For Orientalist authors the literary "flight" to Asia represented more than just a form of escapism, although most literary critics tend to dismiss it as such.[9] Several members of the German intelligentsia had a genuine interest in learning about Asian civilizations, an interest manifested in numerous translations and studies of Asian religious and cultural texts, as well as in actual journeys to the East. Yet the literary use of the exotic Orient gave rise to an ironic situation. For Günther, the great and fascinating paradox of the period before World War I lies in the fact that those who despaired of the ethos of the age directed their search for meaning toward the colonized, exploited East — they sought help from the Other at a time when the phenomenon of alienation was more strongly felt than ever before (12). Authors often expressed an ambivalence toward the Orient which arose out of the paradoxical contrast between the colonial politics of Germany and the intensive exploration of Asian cultures conducted by German intellectuals. Many German authors who wanted to empathize with and relate to Asian cultures maintained a critical stance toward colonialism; but what they actually wrote about the East often revealed their inability to recognize their own submersion in the colonial mentality of the age.

Deeply influenced by Orientalist literary trends, and an admirer of the *1001 Nights*, Hugo von Hofmannsthal wrote the *Märchen der 672. Nacht* (Tale of the 672nd Night, 1895). Here Hofmannsthal explores what he considers to be the magical, mythical aspects of the Orient. The exoticism of the text serves in fact as decoration and as a means for the author to work out and express his ideas about aesthetics: he combines clichéd positive and negative stereotypes about the Orient and seems uninterested in describing any of the historical realities of the region. Rather, claims Wolfgang Köhler, the realities function as a backdrop for Hofmannsthal's dismay at the emotional oppressiveness and the decline of the imperial society in which he lived (50–52).

Similarly, Rainer Maria Rilke's poem "Mohammeds Berufung" (Muhammad's Calling, 1907) discloses a fascination with the Orient, and experiments with a new aesthetic form. By using the structure of a sonnet to tell Muhammad's story, Rilke attempts to synthesize Oriental content and Western form, emphasizing the positive aspects of each, notes Solbrig ("Da" 42). His poem focuses on the most profound experience in the Prophet's life: the moment when Gabriel reveals to him that he will be God's messenger, and Muhammad — until then illiterate — discovers that he can read and recite God's words. The significance of this experience for the entire Islamic world allows Rilke to connect the importance of mystical experience to the power of language so that he can advance his understanding of the role of the artist in society. Although Muhammad's message is excluded from the poem, what apparently appeals to Rilke is what he, as an artist, can exploit about this remarkable figure for his own artistic ends.

Like Rilke, Klabund also tried to advance his particular aesthetic program by telling an Oriental tale. His *Mohammed: Roman eines Propheten* (Muhammad: A Novel about a Prophet, 1917/27) underscores German expressionist desires for universal love, justice, and communion. Although Klabund mentions classical Islamic sources of biographical information on Muhammad, he shows no interest in accurately depicting them; instead, he concentrates on writing an exotic myth to propound his own values and aspirations. According to Solbrig, his depiction of Muhammad conforms to the concerns of German expressionism in two respects: it shows, first, a predilection for exoticisms of all kinds, which corresponds in his Muhammad theme of prophecy to a need for redemption; and second, a readiness to pay homage to a vitalistic figure of power ("Literarischer" 247–48).

By the nineteenth and twentieth centuries several Jewish-German academic Orientalists, among them Ignaz Goldziher, were regarded by Germans as leading authorities on the Islamicate world. As such, they had the respect and attention of European intellectuals in regard to

Oriental matters. Similarly, as prominent Jewish-German authors began increasingly to write Orientalist fiction, their notions about Islamicate cultures influenced German perceptions about the Orient. A representative list of Jewish-German authors and their Orientalist works, along with those by Lasker-Schüler, Wolf, and Werfel, includes: Franz Kafka's "Schakale und Araber" (Jackals and Arabs, 1917), Carl Reinhold Raswan's *Im Land der schwarzen Zelten* (In the Land of the Black Tents, 1934), Joseph Roth's *Die Geschichte der 1002. Nacht* (The Story of the 1002nd Night, 1939), Fritz Wittels' *Der Juwelier von Bagdad* (The Jeweler of Baghdad, 1926), and Arnold Zweig's *De Vriendt kehrt heim* (De Vriendt Returns Home, 1932).

While it was perhaps merely stylish for some Germans in the early twentieth century to experiment with an Oriental aesthetic, the implications of such experimentation were more serious for Jewish-Germans who explored the notion that they themselves might be Orientals. For example, Meir Wiener, a Jewish-German cultural critic, offers the following telling definition of Orientals in an essay from the period:

> Unter 'Orientalen' sind hier neben den *Semiten* jedenfalls auch die Perser und Inder gemeint, unter 'Okzidentalen' die Träger der euro-päischen Kultur, sofern sie die Erfüllung der griechischen ist. (179, emphasis added)

> (It should be understood that, along with the *Semites*, the Persians and Indians come under the rubric 'Oriental'; under the rubric 'Occidental' come the bearers of European culture in so far as it is the culmination of Greek culture.)

Some assimilationist Jews wished to counteract this idea, because they did not want to be perceived as different from non-Jewish Germans. Some Zionists, on the other hand, welcomed and celebrated the notion, because they wanted to preserve a unique cultural identity within German society. In Central Europe great debates arose between Zionists and assimilationists, between Eastern and Western Jews, and between Jewish and non-Jewish intellectuals who, depending on their ideological agendas, either accepted or rejected the idea that Jews were Orientals. Whereas some Zionists — and, ironically, anti-Semitic Germans — claimed that both the *Ostjude* and the *Westjude* were united by a common Oriental heritage, assimilationists indignantly maintained that Jewish-Germans were proudly, thoroughly Western, and therefore were superior to Eastern Jews. The supposed differences between the *Westjuden* and *Ostjuden* are illustrated in a description of the two groups provided by Fabius Schach, a Jewish-German cultural critic at the turn of the century: the Eastern Jews are depicted as Orientals — passionate, wild, spiritual, vivacious, but in need of structure — whereas the Western Jews are rational, civilized, secular, stagnant, and in need of rejuvenation (583–84). Steven Aschheim explains that the images of Jews presented by German society were often debated in Jewish-German discussions. Although it is true, he asserts, that ultimately the German *völkisch* representation of Jews was used to describe both the assimilated and the unassimilated Jew — they were joined because they were perceived as possessing in common a grasping materialism, a want of ethics, and a lack of creativity — there were differences in the stereotypes. The "caftan" or Eastern Jew embodied a mysterious past, the "cravat" or Western Jew pointed to a frightening present; the *Ostjude* was too primitive, the *Westjude* too modern. It was the role of German racism to fuse this apparent dichotomy by uniting the two kinds of Jews in an indivisible fashion, Aschheim suggests (76). It likewise, and paradoxically, became one of the aims of Zionism to unite a fragmented European Jewry to counteract German anti-Semitic stereotypes.

The emergence of the Zionist movement in Central Europe played a major role in bringing to the fore the debates about the Jew as Oriental. Michael Berkowitz claims that, beginning in 1901 with the start of the Jewish National Fund for the settlements in Palestine, a proliferation of images, advertisements, and calls for money linked Jews and Arabs. Even the most assimilated Jewish-Germans were affected by this, because they could not escape the pervasiveness of the Zionist images. The goals of the Zionists' visual arts campaign were twofold: to shape the national soul of the Jews and to determine the relationship between this cultural identity and the cultures of its coinhabitants — Europeans and Muslims (130, 147). Because Jews could not presume to advance culturally if they were forced to live in an environment that was supposedly inherently alien or even antagonistic to them, where they were also excluded from national traditions and established histories, Martin Buber and other Zionists argued that European Jews needed to return to their roots — in Palestine (133). Their goal was to establish in the minds of European, assimilated Jews (even those who did not agree with Zionism) specific images of the landscape and of the Jewish settlements in Palestine. By 1914, their success at this was so great that the impact of these artistic visions on Central European Jewry had become one of Zionism's greatest achievements (144).

The need of Jewish settlers to find a way to peacefully live in Palestine produced contradictory attitudes toward Arabs in Zionist art. Some Zionists argued that Jews and Muslims culturally complemented each other because of their Semitic links. These Zionists, Berkowitz notes, maintained that Islamicate culture was worthy of respect and should be assimilated along with the Western ideals of the Jewish settlers (148). The dissemination of images of Orientalized Jewish settlers who had adopted some of the Arabs' customs in their new lives reinforced the idea that the two cultures were joined in a beneficial way.

Berkowitz finds this facet of Zionist imagery to be a type of "positive orientalism" (152).

In order to depict Jewish settlers as representatives of positive European, humanist, bourgeois values — in contrast to traditional, anti-Semitic clichés — Zionists frequently resorted to using images which reinforced traditional negative European stereotypes about Muslims. Critics have suggested that this aspect of Zionism mirrors the tactics used by European colonialists to justify their imperialist ventures.[10] Arabs were often depicted by Zionists as nonessential elements of society and were characterized as uncivilized, ill-educated, lazy, and even immoral (Berkowitz 147, 149–50). Indeed, Arabs and Sephardic Jews, who were deemed culturally closer to the Arabs, were often oppressed and relegated to the worst jobs in the Jewish settlements (149, 162). Some Zionists believed that Arabs should be grateful for the efforts of European Jews, who were transforming their purportedly poverty-stricken land into a prosperous one — an attitude that mirrored the kind of imperialist point of view that characterized much of European Orientalism.

According to Berkowitz, Zionism at first contended that Jews would achieve sovereignty in Palestine by bringing with them a progressive, Western culture; the Arabs and the rest of Western Asia would be forced to welcome the Zionists as their friends and superiors. Undoubtedly, the Zionists' presumption of being "guides" for the Arabs can be characterized as a variety of Orientalism: since they were Europeans, these Zionists regarded themselves as culturally superior to the Arabs. Such haughtiness was partially tempered by their earnest aspiration to live in rapport with the Arabs and to win them over (164). Yet Berkowitz notes that even Zionists favorably disposed to Arab culture held a patronizing attitude toward Eastern cultures; for example, Theodor Herzl envisioned building a Jewish hospital in Palestine into which the whole of Asia would pour and which would prepare the way for the eradication of diseases in the Orient (164). No matter how Orientalized European Jews in Palestine became, they would still be in a better position to develop the region than their Arab counterparts simply because of their Western backgrounds. Thus these Jews (the Orientals of Europe) could come to be viewed as insiders by the rest of the world. Shohat, however, remarks that Arabs, because of their inherent Easternness, could not be regarded as true equals to the enlightened Westerners; they also could never be considered as being simply "normal" (132).

In the context of the debates about the relationship of Jews to Western and Eastern cultures, the question arose as to whether Jewish-Germans produced a different "type" of art than non-Jews; that is, a type of art with a distinctly non-Western aesthetic. Both Jewish and non-Jewish cultural critics wrote essays trying to prove that this was the case.

For example, some cultural critics from the period, among them Moritz Goldstein, maintained not only that Jewish art is Asiatic, but also that Jews themselves are more poetically inclined than Westerners, precisely because they are Orientals (Bauschinger, "Ich" 89–90). Echoing and modifying sentiments expressed in the past, these critics argued that Oriental-Jewish art could revitalize a Western tradition grown stale. The consequence of such a line of reasoning was that the Jewish artist was hailed as the opposite of the decadent Western artist. Unfortunately, as Gert Mattenklott points out, one of the dangerous consequences of this line of reasoning was that it played into anti-Semitic sentiments expressed by the German public. In the polemic constellation, the Jew — as guide to the wisdom of the East — is depicted as a cultural critic of Western modernism, which *völkisch* ideology also criticized. Yet this strategy ironically also appeared to bolster anti-Semitic stereotypes in that it helped to propagate the image of Jews in Germany as outsiders (299).

Jewish art was partially defined by Jakob Wassermann's essays "Der Literat oder Mythos und Persönlichkeit" (The Literary Figure, Or Myth and Personality, 1909) and "Der Jude als Orientale" (The Jew as Oriental, 1918), as well as a collection of essays by other Jewish-Germans entitled *Juden in der deutschen Literatur* (Jews in German Literature, 1922). These influential texts grapple with the paradox of Jewish-German authors being both marginalized in and central to German culture. They also explore Jewish ties to Western and Oriental cultures. For example, Mattenklott demonstrates that many cultural critics borrowed Nietzsche's categories of the Dionysian and the Apollonian and applied them to the *Ostjuden* and the *Westjuden*, respectively. In any case, he asserts, the meaning of Eastern Jewish vitality is to be interpreted as a manifestation of the Oriental-Dionysian, whose powerful energies bring Western civilization necessary refreshment; this interpretation is the result of the efforts of young Zionist intellectuals around 1900 to explain Nietzsche in the interests of national Jewish emancipation (296–97).

Wassermann, for the most part forgotten now, was considered in his day to be as important a thinker as Thomas Mann. In his essays Wassermann propounds the theory that, because of their tragic history of oppression and assaulted traditions, Jews have developed split personalities. Wassermann describes the European Jew as possessing either — and sometimes both — Western and Eastern characteristics: he is either the most godless or the most godly of all humans; he is either truly socially conscious — be it in archaic, stagnant ways, or in new, utopian ways which destroy the old — or he wants to find himself through anarchic loneliness; he is either apathetic or fanatic, mercenary or prophetic (28). In order to reconcile the polarities, Wassermann argues, the Jewish people have become a type of *Literatenvolk* (literary people). Jewish writers, he explains, are of two types: the Jew as

European, as cosmopolitan, is a literary type; the Jew as Oriental — not in the ethnographic, but in the mythical sense — as someone who makes the transformative power of the present a condition for art, can be a creator (29). The Jew as European, Wassermann continues, is an assimilator who follows trends, has forgotten his history, and believes in the dichotomy between "us" and "them" (29–30). The Jew as Oriental is secure in his identity because he recognizes both his roots and his historical function in Europe as a bridge between Western and Eastern cultures. Because of this, Wassermann sees for these Oriental Jews, and especially the authors among them, a special purpose in contemporary German society. He claims that, as in all eras of great upheaval, a wondrous longing for the East was sweeping across Europe as prophetic minds foretold renewal emanating from the East. He believes that the Jew — the representative and also fictional Jew, the bearer of a worldview which is neither merely quietly creative nor chaotically destructive but has wide-ranging influence — is called on to play a role in this transformation (32). Wassermann's intention is to synthesize his vague sense of Jewish Orientalism with the German *völkisch* soul, with which he very much identified (Mosse, *Beyond* 37–38).

Many of the essays in the important volume *Juden in der deutschen Literatur* argue that Jewish writers express an Oriental (that is, religious, passionate, unrestrained) style and perspective in their works, but that they fuse this with Western (worldly, intellectual, highly crafted) sensibilities. For example, Meir Wiener believes that Oriental authors decorate their literature ornately and excessively — they are Romantics in the deepest sense of the term; whereas the Occidental writers depict their experiences exactly as they are — they strive for reality. The Oriental, Wiener continues, is an aesthete, hence his talent for depicting the transcendent; the Occidental has to learn from the Oriental about the nature of God, because his knowledge of God is muted by his measuredness. In short, the Eastern artistic form wants to veil itself, close itself off from, and turn its back to the world, while the Western form wants to reveal itself and face the world; the first wants to adorn without purpose, the second wants to purposefully expose (180–81). In a similar vein, Erwin Poeschel describes Wassermann's literary style as presenting a perfect illustration of an epoch of Western civilization resting on currents from the distant East, which will perhaps bring with them tomorrow's revitalization (99). Alfred Wolfenstein echoes such a characterization of Jewish literature in his essay "Das neue Dichtertum des Juden" (The New Poetry of the Jews) when he proclaims that a renewal of literature has begun in the West:

> Es ist Frühling im Abendlande. Die Dichtung mit zwei Gesichtern singt Untergang und Aufgang. Vielleicht verkündet sich hier eine Vereinung von Orient und Occident. (357)

(Spring has arrived in the West. Poetry with two aspects [a German one and a Jewish one] sings of decline and emergence. Perhaps a union between the Orient and the Occident is being heralded.)

Such critics never challenge German commonplace understandings of the differences between Oriental and Occidental cultures. Instead, as Gustav Krojanker — the editor of the collection — suggests, the purpose of these essays is first to describe the difficulty Jewish-Germans have in being Oriental Westerners and then to initiate a discourse in which Germans see Jews as fellow citizens and value them precisely because they are different (12). The argument made by the supporters of the categorization of Jews as Orientals is that Jewish-Germans should be admired for representing the best of Eastern and Western cultures.

Many Jewish-German artists turned to expressionism as a way of resolving their Jewish-German and Eastern-Western dichotomous dispositions. German expressionism was about venting pain and suffering, challenging notions of ugliness and Otherness — things preferably ignored by a bourgeois society professing to be comfortable with itself — in order to demonstrate the need for Germans to create a newer, healthier, more honest and inclusive society. Its experimentation with revolutionary forms, mixing the exotic with the familiar, reflected its revolutionary ideals. It sought to force Germans to see and think in new ways: to stretch their imaginations and collapse their preconceptions. Expressionism's artistic program thus reverberated with the historical experiences and modern desires of Jewish-Germans.

Else Lasker-Schüler, Friedrich Wolf, and Franz Werfel were Jewish-German expressionist artists. The fact that they were artists, in and of itself, presents another set of complicated identity issues. According to Sander Gilman, the role of the artist is to eliminate the gap between the artist's realization that the world is in constant flux (chaos) and the need to have a sense that there is a fixed order (meaning) in their lives. The tension arising out of these conflicts causes the artist to create a work of art which simultaneously defines the artist, the audience, and culture. A work of art, therefore, does not necessarily depict what an artist, audience, or society is actually like, but how the artist desires them to be seen (*Other* 1–2, 6, 9–10).

If Lasker-Schüler, Wolf, and Werfel were playing this role as Jewish-German artists, they were doing so from a rather peculiar position vis-a-vis the rest of German society. On the one hand, they were read and respected widely in the German-speaking world and, as such, actively participated in shaping German culture. On the other, due to their Jewish identity they were classified as outsiders by the mainstream, non-Jewish German majority. They were what Edward Said calls "border intellectuals." Border intellectuals are those intellectuals and artists whom society sees as both marginal and central to its culture. JanMohamed —

expounding on Said's concept — explains that their mission is one of establishing for themselves a fixed identity and position in society. And yet, the predicament of the border intellectual is this: how does one establish oneself on a border? In theory and even in practice, borders are neither inside nor outside the territories they delineate; they simply indicate the differences between the two. As mere designators of difference, borders are not spaces at all. Hence intellectuals situated on these sites are not able to straddle a border; instead, they are compelled to constitute themselves as the border. By knowingly or unknowingly composing themselves in this way, border intellectuals "have to guard themselves against the traps of specularity, for the border only functions as a mirror, as a site defining the identity and homogeneity of the group that has constructed it" (JanMohamed, "Worldliness" 102–3). The quandary confronting artists like Lasker-Schüler, Wolf, and Werfel consists of their attempt to determine where the borders between cultural groups lie and how they fit into German society. As border intellectuals, they occupy the place where a culture's "sutures" — which have held together a culture's sense of its homogeneity — have ruptured. Thus the border intellectual who is willing to examine his or her own identity has access both to the values and norms of the larger society and to its alternative prospects (115). As border intellectuals depicting a culture considered to be Other by Germans, Lasker-Schüler, Wolf, and Werfel reveal both the cultural judgments of the majority society of which they are a part and in which they live, and the alternative interpretations of the minority groups to which they also belong.

The waterworks plant for the Sansscouci Palace
in Potsdam, Germany, built in 1842.
(Model of the Alhambra mosque in Grenada, Spain.)
Photo by V. Schubel, 1991.

3: Else Lasker-Schüler's Oriental Performance Space

ELSE LASKER-SCHÜLER WROTE *Die Nächte Tino von Bagdads* (The Nights of Tino of Baghdad, 1907) and *Der Prinz von Theben* (The Prince of Thebes, 1912) out of complex motives.[1] Because Germans understood the Orient as the land of the Other, Lasker-Schüler used it as the setting where her difference could be taken for granted, explored, and then celebrated. The Orient became the space where she could define her role as an artist, a Jew, a unique individual — and be accepted by German society for it.

Else Lasker-Schüler's life began rather unremarkably, but it quickly became extraordinary.[2] She was born into a bourgeois, assimilated but devoutly Jewish-German family in Elberfeld, Germany. What made her an Other in German society, Lasker-Schüler believed, was that she was a misunderstood, mystical visionary. She sensed that she was special early in her life. Being unique, though, was a double-edged sword for her: it produced in her a sense of great pride, but also perhaps an even greater sense of lonesomeness. Growing up as a gifted, sensitive, Jewish child in the Wuppertal, she was perceived as an outsider by her schoolmates. Her feeling of isolation was compounded when her parents, having discovered that she suffered from a form of epilepsy, decided to school her at home. This led Lasker-Schüler to look for role models who had experienced the same alienation she did. In the Biblical figure of Joseph, Lasker-Schüler found someone with whom she could identify and whom she admired; she related to Joseph's having been initially shunned by society, and marveled at the fact that he had nonetheless managed to become a hero through his ability to look into people's souls and interpret their dreams.

In 1894 she married Bertold Lasker — a bourgeois physician — and they moved to Berlin, where she became involved with the literary and art scenes. Bertold was an assimilated Jew who believed in the ideals of the Enlightenment and used them to ensure his acceptance by German bourgeois society. They were divorced by 1900 due to personal and political differences. Since coming to Berlin, Lasker-Schüler had increasingly turned her back on the values of bourgeois German culture: she became a bohemian and a central figure in avant-garde literary and art circles. Although she shunned party politics, her sympathies lay with the oppressed, and therefore to the left. The clubs and cafés she frequented hosted a clientele of anarchists, pacifists, humanists, socialists, feminists and the newly-formed, leftist *Grün Deutschland* (Green Germany) movement, which rejected the middle-class social and moral foundations of Wilhelminian German culture. She gave birth to an illegitimate son by an unknown father, and helped establish the renegade, expressionist literary journal *Der Sturm* (The Storm) with Georg Lewin, whom she renamed Herwath Walden. She married Walden, an assimilated Jew who was a socialist; they divorced in 1911, again due to personal differences. Lasker-Schüler became celebrated, and hence sometimes despised, as the bohemian German artist *par excellence.*[3] Despite her fame, she lived much of her life after her second divorce in dire poverty, sometimes eating next to nothing and sleeping in hallways for days. Although she would have preferred not to have been obliged to constantly beg friends and admirers for hand-outs, she thought that living comfortably would ruin her art. She was, in many ways, a rebel with an artistic cause.

By the time Lasker-Schüler died, some of the most influential German-speaking writers — Jews and Christians alike — had proclaimed her, in the words of Karl Kraus, "the greatest lyric poet of modern Germany" and, according to Gottfried Benn, "the greatest lyric poetess that Germany had ever possessed." Hans Cohn praised her as "perhaps the greatest poet the Jews had ever had," and Peter Hille termed her "*the* Jewish poetess . . . the black swan of Israel." These titles mirror how her admirers recognized her dual identity as a Jewish-German: for Kraus and Benn, she was primarily a German; for Cohn and Hille, she was fundamentally a Jew. But Lasker-Schüler was always both. Indeed, as Marion Kaplan contends, Jewish-German women were never regarded in this period as *just* Jews — or just women, middle-class, or any other single thing — but all of these at once, with one or the other of these factors dominating their identity on different occasions (ix).[4] Lasker-Schüler wrote her poetry in German, but because much of it was about her experience of being Jewish, she called it "Hebrew." Yet she never learned the Hebrew language — not even when she later lived in exile in Palestine. Indeed she became intensely homesick there because she was not surrounded by *her* German language. She was proud of being both a German and a Jew.

Lasker-Schüler loved and identified with the stories from the Hebrew Bible and she unsystematically read the Kaballa. The Judaism she practiced was never conventional — it housed holy figures from other religions too — but, she insisted, it was firmly rooted in Jewish traditions. Lasker-Schüler never cared for Orthodox Judaism, but neither did she believe Jews should ever assimilate fully into the majority Christian culture, no matter how attractive it might seem: Jews needed to remember their history. Although her two husbands were politically very different from each other, part of the problem Lasker-Schüler had with them was that they were both culturally assimilated, profoundly secular Germans. Lasker-Schüler's friendships with people representing diverse points of view in the debate about Jews as Orientals placed her in the middle of these discussions; that she tended to disagree with everyone also ostracized her from the debates. She came under attack from some cultural Zionists for her advocacy of a "new Jewish" literature which synthesized Eastern and Western impulses. Yet she also argued bitterly with Martin Buber and his synthetic vision of Zionism, which maintained that Eastern and Western Jews could unite on matters of Jewish interest and thereby unify the best of what the East and West could culturally offer. She believed this was impossible for most Jews because they had such disparate interests; only special people like herself could manage such a synthesis. But the differences Lasker-Schüler had with many of the Jewish-Germans may not have resulted from religious-cultural reasons, rather most of Germany's Jews were bourgeois and rejected her art because it was not. According to Grunfeld, she wrote to Buber, "I hate the Jews, because they disregard my voice, because their ears have grown shut, and because they prefer listening to cretins and jargon. They eat too much, they should go hungry . . . .Are you angry?" Buber replied that she should "love the Jews with anger and yearning . . . . I think one ought to be more concerned with how one hears the world than how one is heard *by* it" (110).

Like her life and ideals, Lasker-Schüler's art was unconventional. Her literature was greatly influenced by the trend of using Orientalist decoration in art. Some critics, such as Dieter Bänsch, argue that Lasker-Schüler, like other avant-garde artists of her time, used Oriental decoration in her works simply because it was fashionable (65–66). Similarly, Jakob Hessing maintains that it is not the spirit of the Orient which finds expression in Lasker-Schüler's poetry, but rather the spirit of her times (136). Both *Die Nächte Tino von Bagdads* and *Der Prinz von Theben* are collections of short stories reminiscent of the *1001 Arabian Nights*, which was popular at the time.[5] A great admirer of Goethe, Lasker-Schüler used the Orient — like Goethe in his *West-östlicher Diwan* — as the setting for her own artistic exploration of the origins of poetic language and attempted to overcome the limitations of her native tongue. She, too, sought non-Western inspiration in hopes of finding new possibilities for expression. The old tired *Volk* could no longer give Lasker-Schüler what she had sought from the beginning and finally found in her Oriental fantasies: a new language.[6] As a result, she became known as a Jewish-German artist whose poetry, according to the expressionist playwright Erich Mühsam, "glowed with the fire of oriental fantasy," notes Grunfeld (97).

Lasker-Schüler used German creatively and even concocted her own Oriental language, making her unique among authors who used Orientalist decoration in their works. For example, she believed she could speak a language she called *Asiatisch* (Asiatic). It is this "Asiatic" language that she used occasionally in her Orientalist literature. It resonated with Arabic, Turkish, and Hebrew sounds and appeared convincing to nonspeakers of those languages: Lasker-Schüler was actually arrested in a church in Prague for giving a sermon in her *Asiatisch*. The phrases "cha machalaa" (DN 63) and "abbarebbi . . . lachajare. Hu hu uu . . . " (DP 133) echoed some Arabic words. "Machalaa" sounds like "mashallah," which in Arabic approximately means "God willing." Similarly, "Hu" (meaning "He") is the final syllable in "Allahu" and is used in Sufi chants. But her "Asiatic" phrases are otherwise unintelligible. The importance of this "language" to Lasker-Schüler, however, lay in her wish to trace poetic language back to its roots; she believed that this language which she invented approximated a wild, ancient, original language. This wild language corresponds to her interest in approximating the language of the Biblical Jews, whom she calls the *Wildjuden* (wild Jews). It also reflects the general notion which, according to Mattenklott, was popular in Germany since the late 1800s, that the East is the site of the original source of all life (299).

Her experimentation with what she considered to be Orientalized German was even more complex. She uses neologisms peculiar to her own Oriental style describing, for example, Eastern eyes as "Sichelaugen, mandelgoldene, zimtfarbene, Schwärme von schillernden Nilaugen" (crescent-eyes, almond-golden, cinnamon-colored, swarms of shimmering Nile-eyes) (DP 102–3). She also subverts syntactical structures, thus turning prose into poetry: "Alle goldenen Bilder küßten die Moschee, da sie den Derwisch gebar" (All the golden images kissed the mosque, because it gave birth to the dervish) (DP 102). In addition, she converts language into a kind of dance. The first story in *Die Nächte* is called "Ich tanze in der Moschee" (I dance in the mosque) and the readers are invited to lose themselves in the rhythmic, swirling, visual language of the "Arab" poet Tino. Tino's poetic dance determines the tone for the entire work:

> Eine Sternjährige Mumie bin ich und tanze in der Zeit der Fluren. Feierlich steht mein Auge und prophetisch hebt sich mein Arm, und über die Stirne zieht der Tanz eine Schmale Flamme und sie erblaßt und rötet sich wieder von der Unterlippe bis zum Kinn. Und die vielen bunten Perlen klingen um meinen Hals . . . oh, machmede macheii . . . hier steht noch der Schein meines Fußes, meine Schultern zucken leise — machmede macheii, immer wiegen meine Lenden meinen Leib, wie einen dunkelgoldenen Stern. (DN 59)

> (A stars-old mummy am I, and I dance to the time of the fields. My eye stays solemn, and my arm raises prophetically, and above my brow the dance draws a small flame, and it alternately turns pale and then reddens from the lower lip down to the chin. And the many colorful pearls around my neck clink . . . .oh, machmede macheii . . . .here remains the glow of my foot, my shoulders twitch gently — machmede macheii, my loins continue to sway my body, like a dark-gold star.)

Judith Kuckart explains that in dance Tino experiences a kind of freedom from language-bound conventions and is able to therefore express the inexpressible. Dance takes on a spiritual dimension; as a body language, dance opens the boundary between body and spirit. Whoever dances goes into his or her own temple every day. She further asserts that one can see a relationship between Lasker-Schüler's style of writing and the attempt to escape a specifically Western, Greek, logos-bound culture through dance; her literature reflects another way of thinking, an unambivalent movement against categories where the thinker does not actually think, but creates theater of herself and her language from often inexpressible experiences (82). Although one could certainly deconstruct Kuckart's own stereotypical notions about the nature of Western and Eastern expression, her observations are in line with Lasker-Schüler's intentions. The spirituality of dance lends a religious air to the language Lasker-Schüler uses throughout these stories.

In evoking this religious mood, Lasker-Schüler seems to be manipulating the image and movements of the whirling dervishes, an order of Muslim mystics founded by the great thirteenth-century Persian poet Mevlana Jalaluddin Rumi. With the help of trance-inducing music, the ecstatic dancing of the dervishes whirls them into another state of consciousness, bringing them closer to God. Lasker-Schüler's rhythmic use of sound and language is designed to have a similar effect on the reader. In the passage quoted above, the repetition of the "Asiatic" phrase "machmede macheii" calls to mind the chants of dervishes. Lasker-Schüler invokes this technique to bring the reader into her own esoteric imaginative realm. For Lasker-Schüler, expressionism exists in her own realm beyond time — it is, Kuckart writes, like a militant ecstasy which is awakened when the poet bangs her head against reality (21). By such use of language she attempts to break down the barriers between the reader and herself, and therefore also between the familiar twentieth-century, Western world of the reader and the mysterious, fantastic, Oriental world of her imagination. She thinks in a strange language about another reality and seeks to compel the reader to do so as well.

In the context of the discussion about the supposedly Oriental character of Jews, Lasker-Schüler's interest in experimenting with Orientalism is not surprising. In an intriguing exploration of her artistic merit, Meir Wiener examines what it is about Lasker-Schüler that made Peter Hille proclaim her "die jüdische Dichterin" (the Jewish poetess); in doing so, Wiener evaluates the Orientalism of Lasker-Schüler's art. She begins by saying that, since Lasker-Schüler's works contain the abstract images and tropes similar to those found in Oriental art, her style appears even more Jewish than Heine's (Wiener 186). But, Wiener argues, Lasker-Schüler is really just a dilettante who resorts to the use of stereotypes and clichés because she has no real mastery over the genre (188–89). She cannot pull off the charade, Wiener maintains, because it is neither authentic nor does it speak to a larger audience: that is why Lasker-Schüler's poems are so personal, intimate, and why they presuppose of the reader a similar relationship to her experiences. Mistakenly considered expressive, these experiences — loosely created by weak hands — do not speak to others. They are not equipped with what is needed to prepare the way for understanding. Often they are only amusing little games: funny, endearing, written for a private circle of friends, and therefore not actually art (191–2). Wiener ends her essay by suggesting that Lasker-Schüler's works do not exemplify great Jewish art, not because of her Orientalism, but because she is too much of a dilettante (192). Other critics, for example Hessing, echo this sentiment, claiming that she tried to escape the harsh reality of her Jewish existence by adopting Arab guises, but beyond this, her Orientalism was empty (103).

Wiener blames the influence of Oriental art itself on what she perceives as an epidemic of dilettantism, which, according to her, spread throughout Western art during the early twentieth century. Tragic dilettantism, she claims, is responsible for these most striking traits of contemporary poetry: lack of self-control, moodiness, drollery, unconventionality, vague and exaggerated wants. One can trace this tendency back in part to the rampantly spreading influence of the Oriental spirit, which has a degenerative effect when imported into another, inappropriate environment. The purely Occidental, objectively artistic spirit gives way to a hybrid expression of the Oriental. The realization of such a tendency would mean the end of art, Wiener concludes (191).

Although Wiener clearly accepts standard, European stereotypes about the differences between Western and Eastern art (and therefore devalues the latter, even as she sings its praises), what she finds most offensive is the attempt to integrate the two. This is a strange position for someone who believes that great Jewish art is Oriental and yet does not seem to be comfortable with Jewish-German artists experimenting with Eastern styles. What kind of art should a European Jew produce? Are all Jewish-German authors to be relegated to the status of dilettante? Wiener's conflict on this issue mirrors exactly the kind of identity crisis experienced by Jewish-German authors, including Lasker-Schüler, at the beginning of the twentieth century.[7]

In order to express the goals of a "new Jewish" literature — one which explored her ancient, Oriental roots and distinguished her vision as unique in contemporary Jewish concerns — Lasker-Schüler invented the concept of the *Wildjude*. The "wild Jew" is a poetic metaphor for her longing to return to an ancient, original Jewish culture, because she believed contemporary Jewish culture treated her with disregard. The "wild Jews" are modeled on the great heroes of the Hebrew Bible and are intended to serve for both Jews and non-Jews as proud examples of the Jewish past and as role-models for the future. For Lasker-Schüler they are not only exceptional human beings, but also revolutionary artists, notes Bauschinger ("Ich" 94). For example Jussuf, the *Wildjude* king ("Melech") and hero in *Der Prinz*, creates works of art which are considered "Sehenswürdigkeiten aller Zeiten" (timeless displays) (DP 120). This "wildness," which Jussuf possesses, sets Jews and Muslims (in their "natural" states) apart from Westerners; it is supposed to be an inherently Oriental quality characterized by passion, bravery, and the ability to produce great art.[8]

Lasker-Schüler's choice of personas in both *Die Nächte* and *Der Prinz* is revealing in this regard.[9] Although her first-person narrators are almost always Arabs, her third-person narrators empathetically tell the tales of Jewish characters:[10] she never focuses on Christian characters or adopts a Western persona. The narrative forecloses a discussion between Christians and Orientals; unity is established between Jewish and Arab traditions while Christians are silenced. The rift between the Oriental (that is, Jewish and Muslim) worlds and the Christian world cannot be dissolved through love. Their differences are too fundamental, and because of them, the Christians are defeated in battle. Because they are the ones who have been tamed and weakened, they are broken by the wildness of the Orientals.

The European Christians mentioned in these texts are depicted rather negatively. Lasker-Schüler's negative depiction of Christians expresses her uneasiness with European society. She reverses the roles normally played by Westerners and Orientals in European literature: more commonly the Oriental is seen as feminine, seductive, and dangerous, whereas the European is masculine, rational, and benevolent. However, in both of Lasker-Schüler's Orientalist works, the European assumes the characteristics normally attributed to Orientals. Like the portrayal of Orientals in European literature, which denies Orientals a voice in the discourse about their culture, she silences Christian Europeans in her texts.

For example, the English women in the story "Der Derwisch" (The Dervish), curious onlookers at a pious Muslim ritual in Cairo, are inappropriately, immodestly dressed: "Die zarten Hälse der Abendländerinnen heben sich aus dem Rand ihrer durchsichtigen Kleider . . . ." (The tender necks of the Western women rise up out of the necklines of their see-through dresses . . . .) (DP 101). The English women and other Europeans in "Der Kreuzfahrer" (The Crusader) are beautiful and seductive — indeed, Tino is friends with Christian women and has an affair with a crusading knight — but they are also destructive: "[die] kämpfen mit der Taube Mohammeds, die will meinen Schleier zerpflücken" (they fight with Muhammad's dove, which wants to pluck off my veil) (DP 129). Lasker-Schüler portrays these Westerners as a dangerous threat to the Oriental way of life. Although Tino is attracted to them, she recognizes that their insensitivity to the cultural values of Orientals poses the threat of a disruption in the fabric of her culture.

Lasker-Schüler focuses on how Jews and Arabs share a common, non-Western understanding of the world. She almost never chooses to use a Jewish narrative voice in either of these works. She uses this distance alternately to create sympathy for the Jewish characters in her stories or to be very critical of them. On the one hand, she asserts in "Der Derwisch" that Jews are less fanatical in their religious practice than Muslims: they consider the bloody Muslim rituals of Muharram "ein Greuel" (an atrocity) (DP 102). And yet, while the three Jewish kings in *Der Prinz* are admirable figures, in the story "Tschandragupta" (Chandragupta) Lasker-Schüler also exposes the fanatical orthodoxy of a rabbi who refuses to allow an Indian to worship Jehovah in his temple: the rabbi's daughter "bittet ihren Vater, die fromme Gabe seines Gastes nicht zu verachten; der ehrwürdige Knecht Jehovas aber wendet sein Gesicht" (begs her father not to disregard the pious offerings of his guest; the venerable servant of Jehovah, however, turns his head) (DP 98). And the Jewish sultan in "Der Scheik" (The Sheik) may be a highly educated, fascinating companion for the Muslim ruler, but he is also "kein Menschenfreund" (no friend of humanity) (DP 94). By assuming either an Arab or a neutral, unidentifiable third-person voice but never a Western or a Christian one, Lasker-Schüler could distance herself from her own ethnic identity as a Jew, thereby gaining a more detached perspective on Jewish culture. Yet by adopting an Arab persona, she maintained a common, Oriental bond with her Jewish heritage; assuming a Christian or Western voice would have forced her to identify with a culture which, she believed, had different values than her own. Hence her "new Jewish" art focused primarily on Orientals: Jews, and prominently among these, the *Wildjuden*, Arabs and Turks.

Lasker-Schüler adopted an Oriental persona not only in her prose but also in her actual life — claiming she was born in Thebes (she was not), insisting she could speak Arabic (she could not), and adopting the identities of her fictional protagonists in her dress and correspondence. Scholars have suggested different explanations as to why she lived out her Oriental fantasies: in order to cover up the hardships of her impoverished life; to protest an oppressive German monarchy; to compensate for mental illness; or to overcome the restrictions placed on her as a woman living in Germany at that time. Certainly being an impoverished, leftist, eccentric, Jewish woman artist in Germany at the beginning of the twentieth century made her a marginal figure. Lasker-Schüler became first Tino and then Jussuf, because she did not want to be from the cool, sober, technical, metropolitan world of the twentieth century. Instead, she identified with an ancient world, which she believed she could still remember and the languages of which she wanted to be able to speak. Lasker-Schüler chose an Oriental setting for her works and an Oriental persona for herself in order to show how foreign she felt in German culture.

Dressing as an Oriental or speaking with an Oriental voice in Germany differentiated her not only from non-Jewish Germans but also from assimilated, German-speaking Jews. In the process of writing texts about her difference, she made her body into a text as well. The adoption of the "Arab" persona of Tino allowed Lasker-Schüler to distance herself from German culture. Being "Arab" meant she was not German; this emphasized Lasker-Schüler's marginality in Germany and provided her with a vantage point from which she attempted to create art free of Western social restrictions. This tactic gave her certain advantages, but also alienated her from her own German-speaking culture. In her personal life Lasker-Schüler also adopted the persona of Jussuf, a *Wildjude* who became the Prince of Thebes and whose name is the Arabic (not the Hebrew) equivalent of Joseph.[11] Although only one of the stories in her Orientalist works focuses on him ("Abigail der Dritte" (Abigail the Third)), and although Tino, the Princess of Baghdad, is the major narrative voice in both of these texts, Lasker-Schüler wore the mask of Jussuf in her own life from 1910 until she died in 1945. As Kuckart explains, she led a double life as the Prince of Thebes. Her game of hide-and-seek behind the mask of the prince created a space for the chaotic creativity in her writing. In Eastern costume, her serious artistic game guaranteed — despite all derision from others — exotic untouchability (Kuckart 23).

Lasker-Schüler first adopted the persona of Tino in her real life between 1900 and 1910; however, the name was given to her by Peter Hille. Jussuf — a male name — was the name she chose for herself.[12] The possible significance for Lasker-Schüler of cross-dressing as a man is explained by the cultural critic bell hooks in an interview with Andrea Juno. Hooks claims that for women in this period "it was a form of ritual, of play. It was also about power. To cross-dress as a woman in patriarchy meant, more so than now, to symbolically cross from the world of powerlessness to a world of privilege. It was the ultimate intimate voyeuristic gesture" (Juno 79). She also chose to impersonate a wealthy prince, which allowed her metaphorical access to the wealth and political power she lacked as an impoverished, marginalized woman. But cross-dressing for Lasker-Schüler meant wearing the costume not only of another gender but also of another culture. It is therefore significant that she seemingly chose to enter the "world of privilege" by dressing as an important man yet simultaneously denied herself that figurative position of power by living in German society as an *Oriental* prince.

Why did Lasker-Schüler not adopt Jussuf as her persona in either *Die Nächte* or *Der Prinz*? Perhaps adopting his voice in her literature would have associated her too closely with a specific type of Jewish identity, which she wished to avoid. In the character of Tino, the shunned visionary, poet, and "Princess of Baghdad," she found a tangible model of unconventionality. In the story "Der Großmogul von Philippopel" (The Grand Moghul of Philippopel) Tino becomes the wise advisor of, and poet for, a powerful Turkish king who has grown mute. Tino is put in the position of having to speak for — and therefore represent — the Moghul. "In den großen Saal des Reichspalastes werde ich geführt, dort nehmen Schreiber vom Amte meine erdichteten, wundertätigen Worte auf, und die Staatsmänner bilden einen Chor um mich" (I am led into the great hall of the imperial palace, where official scribes take down my miraculous, fabricated words, and the statesmen form a choir around me) (DN 77), Tino reports; "Und es strahlte die Mondsichel mit dem ersten Stern über Konstantinopel" (And the crescent moon and the first star glowed over Constantinople) (DN 78).[13] The parallel of Tino's experience to that of the Biblical Joseph — her early hero — is unmistakable. But unlike the Pharaoh, the king becomes jealous that Tino, and not he, has turned his country into a success, "und vertrieben werde ich [Tino] aus dem Garten des Reichspalastes . . . und ich deute mein Geschick" (and I am driven out of the garden of the imperial palace . . . and I understand my fate) (DN 80). Her talents misunderstood and unappreciated both here and throughout the texts, Tino is forced to flee for her life. Tino, like Joseph, lives in a state of constant exile, and this mirrors the feeling of being exiled from German society which Lasker-Schüler felt throughout her life.[14]

Like Tino, Lasker-Schüler was forced by her society to play a role not necessarily of her own choosing. Being seen as Oriental by her fellow Germans (Jews and non-Jews alike) was surely a burden to her; but she chose to see her situation as an opportunity to create a rewarding niche for herself. And yet, just because she saw her perceived Orientalness as positive, or at least as an opportunity, does not mean that those who judged her did. Still, she managed to turn criticisms of her life and art into something she could accept: she decided that they resulted from jealousy about her specialness, rather than mere rejection. Nevertheless, unlike Joseph's story, Tino's and Lasker-Schüler's do not necessarily end happily. Tino, like Lasker-Schüler, is an artist who longs to be accepted by society and yet realizes her importance as a liminal figure in it. Liminal figures, as defined by Victor Turner, are people who exist "betwixt and between" those categories ordered by "past and future mundane social existence" (202). They occupy a precarious but important position in society in that they are sometimes regarded as wise or holy, but at other times as crazy or dangerous. This is illustrated in "Der Sohn der Lilame" (Lilame's Son), in which Tino teaches her blue-haired cousin to appreciate his uniqueness; unfortunately, he misinterprets this, takes it to an extreme, and comes to be regarded as a ridiculous freak. Tino understands the difference between making a spectacle of oneself and being appreciated for one's uniqueness. In her own life, however, Lasker-Schüler sometimes crossed the fine line.

For Lasker-Schüler the liminal experience is often one of disjointedness. In order to underscore the liminality of her experience, Lasker-Schüler employed three devices in her texts: she wrote collections of disjointed short stories which fit into no fixed genre, she constantly changed the identity and voice of the narrator in these texts, and she imitated important themes from Sufi poetry, an Islamic literary tradition often evoking liminal subjects. The stories contained within both of her Orientalist works form a collection, as one might find in a book of poetry, rather than a linear story. By writing a text that is neither strictly prose nor poetry, she makes it liminal: just as she made her body a text, she made the text to be like her body. The fact that there are no framed stories, that characters jump forwards and backwards in time, and that stories are episodic rather than continuous contributes to a disjointed and fragmented experience for the reader. Lasker-Schüler thereby helps the reader gain access to what liminal figures experience when dealing with society; this fragmentation also mirrors society's view of the Other.

Through the constant switching of narrative voices, Lasker-Schüler insists in her texts that the reader experience her own often disjointed liminality. In *Die Nächte* and *Der Prinz*, the narrative voice changes from first person (singular and plural) to third person, and the narrator changes from male to female, from old to young, from one geographic location to another. By blurring the lines between things normally considered distinct and even opposite, she undermines fixed notions about categories, challenging the reader to see and experience things from multiple perspectives. As Lasker-Schüler herself did in real life, the reader accordingly participates in a type of multicultural cross-dressing while engaging these texts.[15] The Orient provides the perfect setting where lines can be blurred, since it has often been depicted in European literature as a place where Western categories do not apply. Indeed, the Orient as presented in Lasker-Schüler's literature makes no use of conceptions of time and space. The reader never knows what the historical time-frame for the stories is supposed to be; likewise, geography plays no role in separating cultures, because Lasker-Schüler's Orient is a contradictory, ahistorical, amorphous construct. Ultimately, although she consciously uses stylistic contradictions for the sake of experimentation and boundary-stretching, her uncritical use of conventional views about the Orient nonetheless serves to make rigid the perceived borders between East and West.

Tino, the liminal artist whose voice Lasker-Schüler employs most often in these texts, appears similarly contradictory. In this regard she shares much in common with European depictions of Sufi mystics. Sufis (known in different parts of the Islamicate world as qalandars, malangs, fakirs, or dervishes) are liminal figures in their own societies: Muslims consider them poetic, mystical, androgynous, powerful, and contradictory. Since Europeans tend to view them as defying Western categorization, Sufis are often conveniently used in European literature to epitomize all Orientals. Tino possesses many of the same characteristics as Sufis and embodies various inconsistencies: she is both rich and poor, respected and misunderstood, spoiled and abused, happy and sad, old and young, clothed as a man and as a woman, and, above all, is exceptional because she is a visionary and poet. Jussuf, both in the text and in Lasker-Schüler's adoption of his persona in her actual life, also shares many of these traits. As ideal Sufis, Tino and Jussuf represent solitary, androgynous prophets — which exemplifies Lasker-Schüler's own view of herself as an artist.[16] But here again she resorts to using commonplace views about people she wishes to elevate as uncommon and special — a strategy that proves highly problematic for her message.

In many ways Lasker-Schüler creates in the voice of Tino (and, to some extent, of Jussuf) an echo of the great Sufi poets. These ecstatic, mystical, and often esoteric poets write about the longing they feel for their true love or for their home; their poetic motifs serve as metaphors for the separation from God which Sufis hope to overcome.[17] They accept alienation from society as necessary, and they see their art as a secondary result of their mystical search for God. One of the major themes running throughout both of Lasker-Schüler's Orientalist works is of *Sehnsucht* (longing). Tino is the loving "Dichterin Arabiens" (Poetess of Arabia) (DN 70) whose passions exceed those of others; likewise, Jussuf (in "Abigail der Liebende" (Abigail the Loving) DP 122) sings his songs, as Tino does, from an isolated and distant perspective. In these texts Lasker-Schüler emphasizes the idea that *Sehnsucht* serves primarily as a source for artistic inspiration. Such longing must not be satisfied, for, were it not for her *Sehnsucht*, Tino might have been happier, but she would not have been a great artist. This plight mirrors Lasker-Schüler's feelings about her role as an artist. Hessing claims that, for Lasker-Schüler — never assimilated, always suffering under her complex identity — social redemption meant not an eternal promise, but an eternal longing (127).

By forcing the reader to step inside the shoes of exotic Others and to listen to irregularly varying narrative voices, Lasker-Schüler brings about two reactions. First, she confuses her readers, so that they must rethink what is usually taken for granted. She constantly decenters the reader's position, encouraging the reader to explore with her the fringes of both society and literary tradition. Second, by employing a first-person narrative technique, she evokes a kind of empathy between her readers and the exotic Other in her texts. In this way, Tino serves the same function as Zulima in Novalis's novel *Heinrich von Ofterdingen*: she tries to convince the readers that the Orient is a wonderful place by eliciting in them a new-found appreciation for the Other. Indeed, Lasker-Schüler seems to be echoing the German Romantic tradition, which was also interested in a mythical Orient and, to this end, employed *Sehnsucht* as one of its major themes. Lasker-Schüler empowers those figures who would normally be disregarded as *fremd* (alien), while she simultaneously attempts to convince her readers of the value of the misunderstood artist and visionary for society and art. Tino and her world may seem exotic to Germans, and she may not always receive the respect she deserves in her own culture, but upon her death, "von den Gipfeln der Pyramiden sprechen Priester zu allen Rosenmonaten ihre Märchen, und es ist bald niemand mehr im Lande, der sie nicht kennt" (from the tops of the pyramids, priests tell her fairy tales every Rose month, and soon there is no one in the region who does not know them) (DN 73). By depicting Tino in these ways, Lasker-Schüler promotes her own position as an eccentric, Jewish-German artist living in a German society which, she thought, often failed to recognize her worth — but perhaps might sometime in the future.

One of Lasker-Schüler's goals, which she expresses throughout her Orientalist literature, was to be appreciated as a unique Jewish artist and visionary who was developing a new type of art that bridged the cultural gap between East and West. According to Bauschinger, one of the major themes of Lasker-Schüler's work as a whole is the recognition of the Other, whose exoticism, even while intriguing us with its foreignness, can be transcended in a relationship based on an understanding of art ("Ich" 90). The task of these texts is thus to construct a world that differentiates itself from that of Western reality. The Orient provided her with a space in which she had more room to experiment with her ideas than she believed she could find in Germany, and where she could let her imagination freely wander. It was also a place where she could work out the various facets of her personality and reassure herself that she was a creative woman who was not crazy, but simply different from most Germans. In the Orient that Lasker-Schüler had constructed, she was in control of her situation and could ensure that she received some of the respect she believed she deserved for her talents: she was the esteemed poet Tino and the beloved Prince Jussuf. There, suggests Kuckart, "Im Selbstbewußtsein nah der Eigenliebe werden Dichterkranz und Prinzenkrone zu austauschbaren Insignien ihrer Erwähltheit" (Self-aware, almost to the point of being self-infatuated, laurel wreath and royal crown became interchangeable insignias of her chosenness) (26). If the realities of life in Germany did not validate Lasker-Schüler as she wanted, her fantasy life in the Orient did.

And yet the ramifications of Lasker-Schüler's use of the Orient as a space for the expression of her Otherness prove to be problematic. Although Lasker-Schüler was attempting to exalt her difference — thereby making the marginalized of society its center — she did so by reproducing many of the stereotypes about the Orient found in European literature: it is a place of lascivious sensuality, a realm characterized by inherent violence. Her view of this region is fraught with inconsistencies and racist attitudes, because she was not concerned about understanding or realistically depicting a "historical" place. Over and over, Asia is presented as timeless and contextless, and most Arabs and Turks are described as being overly obsessed with luxury, sex, violence, or all of the above.[18] For example, in "Ein Brief meiner Base Schalome [sic]" (A Letter to my Aunt Shalom) Tino reports the following sadistic harem scene, which incorporates these elements:

> Meine besessene Tante in der überweiten Brokathose beginnt sich zu entkleiden; neugierig folgen die anderen Frauen den Belehrungen des Eunuchen. Ein großes Buch mit grausamen Bildern breitet er auf dem Teppich hin. Seine Stimme schlängelt sich ein lüsterner Bach um die fiebernden Sinne der Frauen . . . . Ich bebe, der Eunuche ergreift eine der vielfältigen Peitschen; in Bleikugeln endet jeder Riemen; er wetzt sie einige Male wagerecht in der Luft, läßt sie dann langsam herab auf den weiten überweiten allerwertesten Vollmond meiner fiebernden Tante prallen, die ihn, ich schwöre es bei Allah, nach allen Seiten hin ihm zuwendet, mörderisch aufschreiend, kokett die Zähne zeigend. (DP 106)

> (My possessed aunt in the overly wide brocade pants begins to undress; with curiosity, the other women follow the instructions of the eunuch. He spreads a book with gruesome pictures out on the carpet. His voice snakes like a lascivious stream around the feverish desires of the women . . . . I tremble, the eunuch grabs one of the various whips; each thong ends with a lead ball; he whets them boldly a few times in the air, and then lets them slowly bounce off the wide, overly wide, very worthy full moon of my feverish aunt, who — I swear upon Allah — turns it to him in every direction, murderously screaming and coquettishly showing him her teeth.)

Lasker-Schüler's descriptions replicated many of those European stances toward the Orient which, according to Said, were rooted, consciously or not, in an ideology of imperialism. Even though Lasker-Schüler was not an imperialist *per se*, her adoption of these stereotypes discloses an assertion of power over the Orient. Indeed, her ability to subjectively define an Islamicate Orient empowered Lasker-Schüler as an artist in a way which she never experienced in the other realms of her life as a Jew living in Germany: she determined how an entire culture —

the Orient produced by her imagination — thought and felt by advancing her own artistic and personal goals. And she could do this because most of her German readers at that time had never been to the East, or uncritically believed German cultural assumptions about that part of the world, or both. For them, as for Lasker-Schüler, the Orient was nothing more than an imaginative space. In fact, when she was forced into exile, Lasker-Schüler worried about going to Palestine because she would have to confront the actual Orient there. She freely admitted that she much preferred "her" Orient (that is, the one she created in her fantasies) over the real one. "She was suddenly terrified at the thought of having to stay in this Near East," writes Grunfeld, "which she had so often evoked in the Arabian Nights of her imagination" (142).

With her use of Orientalism, Lasker-Schüler is not so different from other German artists — like Goethe or Rilke — who thought they were examining different cultural values by experimenting with Orientalism, but were actually exploring themselves. Exoticism says very little about the reality of the foreign world, but it reveals much about one's own world. Tilman Osterwold explains that the European artist needs allegories and symbols to produce meaning where the levels of reference are not entirely clear or comprehensible, where ambiguity exists, or where uncertainty must be compensated for. Cultural generalizations — useful as backdrops or settings — seem to predominate in this situation. Symbolism serves only to reveal European standards and obliterates what is authentic about the alien, what is incalculable and imponderable. Symbols and allegories thrive because ambiguities exist, but the artist attempts to satisfy all aspects of ethical, societal, and aesthetic norms (30). According to Mattenklott, the expressionist author Kurt Pinthus realized this was also the case for Lasker-Schüler, who, he maintained, was not attempting to flee the realities of her world by escaping to a highly ahistorical Orient, but was actually describing and coming to terms with it (330–31).

Because Lasker-Schüler saw herself as an Oriental Jew who was nevertheless firmly grounded in the German literary tradition, her intention in *Die Nächte Tino von Bagdads* and *Der Prinz von Theben* was to create an aesthetic that would bridge the gulf that she believed existed between herself and German society. However, instead of establishing a bond of common humanity between all people in the East and West, Lasker-Schüler emphasized only those aspects of the Orient which could be appreciated by other "special" artists like herself: its exotic, foreign, esoteric nature. In the end, by reproducing those German stereotypes about the Orient which were designed to establish it as totally alien, she further widened the gulf between herself and those from whom she sought acceptance and praise. Sadly, even later in Palestine she continued to feel alienated from European Jews, among whom she lived. In Jerusalem she experienced rejection or, what was even worse, indifference from her cultural peers, just as she had earlier from many Jews in Germany; still, reports Grunfeld, "she consoled herself with the thought that, 'after all, I'm not Jewish for the Jews' sake, but for God'" (143–44). Predictably, perhaps, she believed she found in the Arabs, who also had been proclaimed outsiders in their own land, kindred spirits — "unsere Brüder im Herzen" (our brothers at heart)[19] — even if she did not bother to learn much about either their language or culture.

Selbstportrait (Selfportrait).
Lithograph by Lasker-Schüler, 1913.
Reproduced from Hebräische Balladen.

Der Bund der wilden Juden (Union of Wild Jews).
Lithograph by Lasker-Schüler, 1923.
Reproduced from Theben: Gedichte und Lithographien.

4: An Oriental Role Model for Friedrich Wolf

DESPITE ITS MIXED reviews from critics, Friedrich Wolf's *Mohammed: Ein Oratorium* (Muhammad: An Oratorio) reveals many of the specific concerns of a Jewish-German author attracted to the exotic Orient.[1] Like Else Lasker-Schüler, Wolf turned toward the East in search of solutions to his personal and cultural problems and in order to redefine himself through an exploration of the Other. Yet Wolf reaches very different conclusions from Lasker-Schüler, not only about his identity, but also about his relationship to the Orient.

Wolf began writing *Mohammed*, his first drama, while fighting in the trenches of Flanders in 1917.[2] The play tells the story of Muhammad and his struggle to establish the religion of Islam.[3] Contrary to the older tradition in German literature of depicting Muhammad as a devil or a false prophet, Wolf — like Goethe and Rilke, not so long before him — praised Muhammad for being a prophet and founder of one of the world's major religions and someone whose message nonetheless has universal appeal. Basing his version of Muhammad's biography upon German Orientalist accounts of traditional Muslim sources, Wolf emphasized those incidents which he thought were particularly relevant to the European context in which he found himself: in the middle of the first World War. Wolf depicted Muhammad as especially concerned with peace and justice, both of which eluded Europe (and particularly Germany) at the time. As a Jewish-German medical doctor fighting on the western front, Wolf praised an Oriental prophet — Muhammad — as a role model for Europeans by depicting him as an advocate of nonviolence and antiimperialism. In doing so, Wolf addressed German cultural understandings of the Other while creating empathy for someone outside of both Judaic and Christian traditions. Along with works by Tolstoy, a German translation of the Qur'an was one of the few books Wolf took with him to the front.

Following the lead of other artists and intellectuals of the time, Wolf — who was unable to travel to the Orient — nevertheless intensively studied Hindu philosophy, the *Epic of Gilgamesh*, and the Qur'an before and during World War I.[4] Wolf's play *Mohammed* can therefore be seen as part of the discourse in Orientalist German literature which sought to understand the exotic in order to propose alternatives to what was going on at home.[5] Yet Wolf's depiction of Arabs is relatively free of the stereotypical characterization of Orientals to which many other authors resorted. He never depicted even the "bad"

Arabs as stupid or irrational: all the characters in his play are represented as intelligent people with motives every bit as rational and under-standable as those of any German. Wolf's remarkably unbiased attitude toward his exotic characters seems to reflect a deep-seated respect for Islamicate culture. This respect may also point to something even more significant: a desire on Wolf's part to really learn from the Other.

By the end of the war, Wolf had plenty to criticize about European, and especially German, culture. As a doctor at the front, he had at first been an enthusiastic supporter of the war, but had begun to question the war as early as 1916.[6] The turning point came in 1917 when his friend Paul Bender was killed at his side in the trenches of Flanders. From this point on, Wolf openly criticized the war:

> Auch war ich bis 1917 ein wilder Hurrakrieger und habe dann unter schweren Krisen mein Damascus erlebt und alle Folgerungen daraus gezogen.[7]

> (Until 1917 I, too, was an enthusiastic cheerleader for the war effort. And then, after many horrible crises, I experienced my own Damascus and reached my own conclusions.)

He also began to question the meaning of his life. Wolf had grown up in a social-democratic household, and his experience of the war pushed his politics even further to the left.[8] By the end of the war, he had joined the revolutionary Workers' and Soldiers' Council.

Friedrich Wolf had been raised in a family which had actively reminded him to cherish the accomplishments of Jewish culture and the history of his Jewish ancestors. Given Wolf's interest in Islam, it may be of no little consequence that his ancestors were Sephardic Jews who had emigrated first to the Netherlands and then to the German Rhineland because of the Spanish Inquisition. Living as a Jew in the liberal Rhineland, Wolf was taught to reject thoughtless prejudices, hatred of foreigners, and every form of racism.[9] Wolf attended a Jewish elementary school and, because of his interest in religious issues as a youth, had the intention of becoming a rabbi. And yet, despite the pride instilled in him for his heritage, Wolf officially renounced the Jewish faith in 1913. This caused a falling out with his father. And his favorite uncle — Moritz Meyer — wrote Wolf a series of letters designed to convince him not to renounce his religious roots. In one of the letters, Wolf's uncle reminds him that a four-thousand year-old, Jewish voice rang out in Wolf (Meyer 128).[10]

Wolf remained committed to what he called the ethics and morality of all the world's religions, and not just to Judaism.[11] Despite the eclectic direction his religious convictions took, Wolf still entertained dreams of emigrating to Palestine after the war to work in the Zionist settlement camps. Wolf did not find this a contradictory position; many Jewish-Germans — including agnostics, atheists, and the culturally assimilated — sympathized, and even identified, with the Zionists who had gone to the Levant. While reading the Qur'an, Wolf formulated what he considered to be the universal basis of all religions:

> Wenn wir auch nicht das Größte leisten, aber etwas leisten, was mit der Ewigkeit zusammenhängt, das ist jedem vergönnt. Dieser Gedanke, ins moralische übertragen, bleibt der Grundgedanke jeder Religion.[12]

> (It is everyone's privilege that, even if we do not achieve the greatest connection to the eternal, we still can achieve something of it. This thought, transferred into morality, remains the basis of every religion.)

Later in his life, Wolf implied that he had been working through many issues pertaining to his Jewish heritage, and to his religious beliefs in general, issues which manifested themselves in his interest in Islam and in writing *Mohammed*.[13]

Mohammed traces the Prophet's life from his youth until his departure from Mecca for Medina. In the prologue, a young Muhammad learns from the Syrian monk Bahirah that he will be God's prophet; examples of miraculous events in Muhammad's life and the fact that he has the birthmark of a prophet on his back support Bahirah's claim. In the first act, which takes place many years later, more is revealed about the character and situation of Muhammad. He is a very successful businessman who is criticized for freeing his slaves and giving away his money; he also agonizes about whether he is actually "chosen" or not. He rejects the advice of both Chadidjeh (his employer and future wife), who counsels him to live an entirely worldly life, and Waraka (Chadidjeh's monotheistic cousin), who urges him to live an ascetic one. In the second act, Muhammad's relationship to the citizens of Mecca is explored. Mecca's socio-economic and religious systems are in chaos because the clans which govern the city are no longer cooperating. In one of the intertribal disputes, Muhammad proves himself a fair arbitrator between the clans but is unwilling to become a political figure, for he believes he is simply expressing God's will. He also resists the temptations of an evil *jinn*, who tries to persuade him to misuse his power. In act three God reveals himself to Muhammad on Mount Hira. Muhammad learns to trust in God's will, and his cousin Ali swears allegiance to him as God's prophet. After he returns home, his house is stormed by angry members of a rival clan who claim that Muhammad's teachings about social justice have jeopardized their power; they demand that he recant so that order can be restored. He refuses, repels their violent attacks with nonviolent tactics, and converts people in his own clan in the process; the attackers are driven out of the house. The final act concerns the so-called Satanic Verses and Muhammad's break with Mecca. Resisting pressure from the other clans and reversing a statement he had made earlier, Muhammad refuses to acknowledge that his God is simply one among the other deities worshipped in Mecca.

Instead he tells the Meccans that they must smash the idols and recognize the one, true God, for whom he is the messenger. Although this message is received with hostility from the Meccans, he instantly converts a group of pilgrims from Jathrib (Medina), who then convince him to bring his message to their city. The play ends with Muhammad preparing for his departure in the face of adversity but with the knowledge that God is on his side. In order to maintain his theme of nonviolence, Wolf ends the play before the historical Muhammad becomes involved in armed struggle.

Wolf, like Ernst Toller and other German expressionists, places his hopes on a great individual whose compassion for the oppressed will result in a transformation of society. The form and language of *Mohammed* reflect the style used by other expressionist writers at that time. Wolf rejected the classical form; the play consists of a *Vorspiel* (prologue) and four acts, the third of which is comprised of two scenes. The language is passionate and Angst-ridden, reflecting the "O, Mensch!" (Oh, humanity!) themes common in expressionist drama. For example, when Muhammad and Chadidjeh discuss the possibility of marriage, Muhammad's warning to her about his precarious situation mirrors the pathos and anguish typical of heroes in expressionist drama:

> Begreife dies, Chadidjeh! Nicht besitz ich mich; wie bedarf ich da vergeben, was ich nicht besitze? *Geheimnisvoll.* Ich bin Sklave meiner Träum' und Schatten, die mich bei lichter Helle jagen! Mich jagen Geister, schlimme . . . schlimme; will ich sie denken, weichen sie wie Dunst . . . sag's keinem, keinem . . . Dir nur trau ich's! Die Furcht, mich zu enthüllen, meine Not, das ist mein Hochmut! *Bäumt sich in Qual.* O fliehe mich, Chadidjeh! Ich bin ein Besessener! (I.30)

> (Understand this, Chadidjeh! I don't belong to myself; how can I give away what I don't own? *Mysteriously.* I'm a slave to my dreams and shadows, which chase me in bright daylight! Ghosts chase me . . . terrible, terrible; when I try to conceive of them, they vanish like mist . . . tell no one, no one . . . I trust only you! My fear of revealing myself, my need to do so, that is my arrogance! *Quaking with agony.* Oh, flee from me, Chadidjeh! I am possessed!)

Reflecting his later literary concerns, in 1951 Wolf reedited *Mohammed* in order to strengthen some of its political implications and to weaken its mystical, religious ones. For example, he substituted the epigraph "Willst du kein Sklave sein, steh auf!" (If you don't want to be a slave, rise up!) for the one used in the earlier versions — "Wer kann schweigen, wenn die Seele brennt!" (Who can remain silent when their soul is on fire!). Thus the emphasis of the play later shifts from issues of truth and individual action to class struggle. However, Wolf did not make any significant additions to the play; this quote about slavery already existed in the earlier version. Instead he deleted sentences and even whole sections, occasionally changing some of the words. On balance he deleted a fair amount of the hyperbolic, expressionistic language as well as references to the importance of recognizing God's will. Gone, therefore, are such phrases as "there is no knowledge without revelation!" (51).[14]

The biography of Muhammad that Wolf recounts is derived chiefly from versions provided by the two turn-of-the-century German Islamicists Wolf was reading at the time, Max Henning and Friedrich Delitzsch.[15] Henning and Delitzsch were not unanimous in their conclusions about Muhammad. Henning, like Delitzsch, talks about Muhammad's humble beginnings, his connection to the Judeo-Christian tradition, his intelligence and diplomatic skills, and his appeal to those seeking social justice. However, Henning paints a more negative picture than Delitzsch, as he also accentuates the conflicts between Muhammad and various Jewish communities and implies that Muhammad became rather power-hungry (25).

Delitzsch, though, emphasizes that Muhammad was a conqueror capable of the greatest gentleness (747). He laments the fact that Muhammad is misunderstood in the West as a false prophet (66), and praises him as a great reformer of the customs of both pagan Arab and Judeo-Christian cultures. Writing in 1915, Delitzsch explains that his motivation for providing such a sympathetic account of both Muhammad and his message stems from the fact that the Germans are allies of the Turks, and they therefore have a duty to understand Islam. He claims it is imperative that the Germans appreciate Islamicate culture so they can better comprehend why the British and the Russians' "Eroberungsgier" (greed for conquest) must be prevented from further colonization of the Muslims (8–9). Whether Wolf agrees with this line of argumentation or not, he certainly praises Delitzsch. In a letter to his mother, Wolf describes Delitzsch as a sensitive and learned authority and enthusiastic friend of Islam and endorses Delitzsch's book as a historically-based presentation of Muhammad's teachings and of the Qur'an in particular; he advises his mother to buy the book.[16]

These German Orientalist scholars based their accounts of Muhammad's life upon traditional Muslim sources,[17] and Wolf's drama faithfully recreated the life of the Prophet in a way which was praised by at least one Muslim contemporary of the playwright's — Said Imam of Damascus.[18] Throughout Wolf's letters and diary entries at the time he was writing the play, it is clear that Wolf wanted to depict Muhammad in as accurate and positive a light as possible. Nevertheless, Wolf occasionally heightened the dramatic effect of the story. For example, he created conversations which are not found in the traditional sources, but are essential for giving voice to Muhammad's personal struggles on stage. Wolf invented a conversation between Chadidjeh and Muhammad on Mount Hira, in which they discuss the conflict between their relationship and his loyalty to God. It pains Muhammad to inform her that his love for her cannot be as central to his life as his love for God: "Ihm gab ich mich seit Mond und Sonnen, ihn harrte ich in letzter, ungeteilter Liebe . . . . Vertraut [sic] dein Herz . . . verlaß mich!" (I have been giving myself to him for ages. With lasting and indivisible love I awaited him . . . . Trust your heart: leave me!) (III.48). This dialogue serves to illustrate the inner struggle Muhammad faces in balancing his worldly concerns with the spiritual demands on him as God's prophet. Similarly, Wolf develops the dramatic motif of Muhammad being the "Lion of God" — a motif which Muslims usually associate with Ali, rather than the Prophet. Wolf was attracted to this image because the lion is majestic and powerful, attributes important for the messenger of God. Thus Bahirah urges the people of Mecca to follow the lion of God (Muhammad) in the beginning of the drama (16); and at the end, when the rival clans still refuse to believe him, Muhammad is transformed into a wrathful lion before whom they disperse like lambs (IV.67). This image underscores Muhammad's function as the medium for God's judgment: unprovoked, he reflects God's love and patience; provoked, he reveals God's wrath. However, unlike the historical Prophet, Wolf's Muhammad never commits an act of violence: Wolf ends the play before we see Muhammad engaged in violent struggle against his enemies.

These additions to Muhammad's story serve to enhance the project of the drama, which Wolf described as an exploration of the integrity of a great man who meets the challenge of his fate.[19] Wolf, who had been "fated" to fight in a gruesome war, was keenly intrigued by the personal qualities of Muhammad which helped him to persevere under difficult circumstances. Muhammad became a role model for Wolf, who focused on those traits in the Prophet which he considered universally admirable. Muhammad is depicted as an intelligent, decent person who becomes a prophet. He exhibits all the characteristics of a German Romantic *Genie* (genius): he is a passionate, tortured loner who is both poetically gifted and a remarkably utopian thinker. The people of Mecca do not know what to make of him. They wonder if he is a magician, a poet, or — in a wonderful play on the concept of *Genie* — is merely possessed by a *jinn* (genie) (IV.60). Unlike the typical German Romantic literary concept of the *Genie*, Muhammad is also very human, struggling with his decisions and hoping to live up to God's expectations. Just as he has an otherworldly aspect, he is also very much concerned to live in and change the material world around him; when Waraka tries to convince him to renounce secular life, Muhammad rejects this, concerning himself with practical things — like making a living (I.22–23). Muhammad is decidedly egalitarian. He chastises Waraka for referring to the Meccans as a swarm of mosquitos and telling Muhammad that he is better than they (I.23). For someone who is so rooted in spiritual experience, Muhammad is anything but wholly otherworldly. Because he has practical as well as religious concerns, he declares that the godliest type of person is a man who does good deeds (I.28).

In keeping with this philosophy, Muhammad sees the purpose of being a prophet as including being a successful and active person whose message and deeds eventually transform the world: "Bin ich Prophet, so werdet Gläubige! Doch nicht im Stein und Zeichen, nein, im Herzen!" (If I am a prophet, then become believers! But not just in name only, no, but with your whole hearts!) (IV.69). This makes him markedly different from the tragic heroes of expressionist dramas, who are usually defeated by forces of ignorance or evil. Instead of being merely an inaccessible, "chosen" person, the character of Muhammad also becomes someone all people should try to emulate.

In the play, Muhammad's political message focuses on three primary areas of concern: a demand for social justice for the oppressed, an advocacy of nonviolent solutions to conflict, and a critique of the materialism which produces imperialistic behavior. Muhammad propounds these positions at a time when the greed of Mecca's powerful clans has led to conflict between them which, in turn, has led to political and social chaos. Wolf underscores this situation in the second act by drawing on an event described in classical Islamic sources: the intertribal conflict over the Kaaba. Each of the clans wants the sole honor of moving the holy black stone in order to bring blessings on them, and each is prepared to fight with the others to get it (II.32–33). Muhammad finds a way for them to cooperate and together move the stone, but they do not understand the lesson he is trying to teach them. He explains the lesson to Ali: "Doch da wir an uns selbst das Gut nur ehren, nicht das Gute" (Because we only value our material goods, and not what is good in us), we mistakenly dwell on how to acquire more wealth instead of thanking God for our existence (II.36–37). This blind materialism results in a lack of regard for the value of other people's lives; this posture leads to slavery and violence.

Muhammad values the well-being of others over his own material gain. He explains to the incredulous Chadidjeh that he has freed his slaves, because he could not have them risk their lives defending his caravans — which actually belong not to him, but to her — on dangerous journeys. He tells her that a single drop of blood from the left hand of a slave means more to him than all the wares in the caravan, and that he only takes into account the lives of the slaves, nothing more (I.22–23). Muhammad's action angers the wealthy Meccans, who recognize it as a potential threat to the social order. He is accused of harming the social structure, to which he replies that they know nothing about the poverty of their people (III.56). He has given the slaves hope, and the slaves approach him to ask him to free all the slaves in Mecca.

They tell him them want to be free so that they can become wealthy (III.42). Muhammad explains that this is not the point of freedom:

> MOHAMMED STEINERN: Willst du kein Sklav sein, so steh auf! Niemand braucht Sklav sein, der sich nicht selbst betäubt; niemand kann frei sein, der sich nicht selbst erlöst!
>
> ZWEITER [SKLAVE]: Du spottest, Herr! Wie sollen wir uns selbst die Nacken lösen, da unsere Säckel leer und unsere Lenden schwertlos?
>
> MOHAMMED: O ihr Volk, ihr wißt nur was ihr wünscht und nicht was not! Nicht gilt's die Nacken lösen, eh ihr die Herzen nicht gelöst von Blutdurst, Wahn und Gier! Dann fielen eure Ketten, ihr rächtet euch an euren Herren und knechtet die Verhaßten, und wär't ihr reich, gleich werbt ihr neue Sklaven und schindet sie aufs Blut um eurer Macht!
>
> (III.42)

> (MUHAMMAD, STONY: If you do not want to be a slave, rise up! No one has to be a slave who does not put himself in the dust; no one can be free who does not save himself.
>
> SECOND SLAVE: You are making fun of us, sir! How can we liberate ourselves when our purses are empty and we have no swords?
>
> MUHAMMAD: Oh people, you only know what you wish for and not what you need. Liberation means nothing if you do not first liberate your hearts from revenge, delusions, and greed! If your chains were to fall away, you would take revenge on your masters and subjugate those you hate; and if you were to become rich, you would immediately enlist new slaves and work them to death for the sake of your own power.)

Muhammad wants to change the mindset of the people, and not just have them reverse roles; otherwise, there is no real possibility of realizing justice. Muhammad's analysis of the slaves' situation hinges on the belief that it is primarily their perspective which needs to be changed, not necessarily their material conditions. This stance indicates that, while Wolf's antibourgeois sympathies were left-leaning, he certainly had not yet adopted a Marxist perspective.[20]

Muhammad has to face the consequences of his radical position vis-a-vis slavery when the slaves threaten violent revolt. He is accused by the Meccans in act three of having told the slaves to revolt, and the rival clans storm his house. He responds to their charges by telling them he rejects violence — the slaves have misunderstood his revolutionary message (III.54). A fight breaks out, and Muhammad refuses to physically defend himself: "Ich brauche nicht die Faust, ich brauche . . . den . . . Willen . . . ." (I do not need the fist, I need . . . the . . . will . . . .) (III.58). The fact that he remains nonviolent even when he is in danger deeply impresses one of his clansmen, who breaks up the fight and proclaims Muhammad the strongest amongst them (III.59). His insistence upon using nonviolent means to resolve conflicts reinforces his message about valuing life and, therefore, God's creation. Since Muhammad believes he is only relaying God's will, it is also clear that God does not condone violence.

Ultimately, Muhammad condemns violence and the oppression of others as symptoms of a poverty of soul: the more people want, the more they will resort to oppression and violence, and the less fully realized they become as humans. In a key scene, Muhammad sums up the outcome of rampant materialism in a debate with the wealthy leaders of Mecca:

> MOHAMMED EISERN: . . . zuviel habt ihr und langt im Vielen nach dem mehr, jagt euch den kleinsten Vorteil ab, Klugheit wird List, List wird zur Tücke, Kraft Gewalt, Gewalt wird Vergewaltigung, Fehde wird, Blut rinnt, Geschlechter morden sich und aus der Jagd nach Mehr wird endlich nur das große Grab des Nichts!

> ABU DJAHL: Lammsgeblöck! Ein starkes Volk braucht Land und Macht, so wie der Leib die Nahrung, sonst's leidet's Not!

> MOHAMMED AUFFLAMMEND: Not! Wüßtest du, woran wir leiden! Die Not des Volkes, das ist die Not der Herzen! Wähnt nicht das Volk zu stillen mit Land und Brot, mit Schwert und Gold! Nicht wieviel es braucht an Macht und Habe, wie wenig es bedarf, um groß zu sein, ist eines Volkes Maß! Seht hier zwei Schalen einer Wage! Auf einer lieget Gold, Land, Krieg, Macht, Blut und Frevel, doch auf der andern euer Herz in Armut und in Einfalt; seht das Gesetz der Wage: eine Schale kann nur steigen, wenn die andere sinkt! Darum vernehmt's, was ihr nicht hören wollt, daß Armut Reichtum, daß eines Volkes Herz mit Macht ihr weder stillt, noch fesselt!

>   (III.56–57)

> (MUHAMMAD, RESOLUTELY: . . . you already have too much and yet you reach for more; you hunt down the smallest advantage, cleverness becomes cunning, cunning becomes spite, power becomes violence, violence becomes rape, feuds start, blood flows, clans kill one another, and the race for more finally ends in the great grave of nothingness!

> ABU JAHL: The bleating of a lamb! A strong people needs land and power — just as the body needs nourishment — or else it suffers from need!

> MUHAMMAD, FIERY: Need! How would you know what we are suffering from? The despair of the people is the despair of the heart! Do not imagine you can subdue the people with land and bread, with swords and gold! One measures a people not by how much power and how many possessions it needs, but by how little it needs to be great! Look at the two sides of this scale. On the one side lies gold, land, war, power, blood, and crimes; and

on the other lies the heart in all its poverty and simplicity.
Behold the law of the scale: one side can only rise when the
other falls! Therefore hear what you do not want to hear: that
poverty means wealth, that you can neither forcibly silence nor
shackle the people's heart.)

In a direct manner, Muhammad's plea for peace and justice becomes an
indictment of the imperialism which results from unbridled materialism.
He argues that expansionist goals lead to unjust wars in the short run
and the self-destruction of people in the long run.

Clearly the contentious tribalism and violence of Mecca in
Muhammad's time mirrors for Wolf the situation in Europe before and
during the First World War. In letters to friends and family written during
this period, Wolf draws parallels between the themes in *Mohammed* and
the conclusions he reaches about the war and Germany's position in it.
For example, on the subject of imperialistic German war-aims, he writes
that all of the Germans' expansionist desires lead to suicide. He explains
why he wrote in *Mohammed* "A people is measured not by how much
it craves and holds onto, but rather by how little it needs in order to be
great": for Wolf, imperialist expansion comes at the expense of depth,
and political maneuvering for power comes at the expense of inner
strength and ethics.[21] Wolf rejected the violence of the war, and became
a pacifist in 1917 — for which he was temporarily sent to a sanatorium.
As a doctor and a soldier, he saw for himself that the greed for
expansion by countries, fed by the materialism of their citizens, led only
to death and destruction.

Wolf's critique of the war, and the attitudes that produced it,
developed primarily out of his own tragic personal experiences, as well
as out of his intensive study of Tolstoy and the Qur'an. Wolf decided
that he had much to learn from the Prophet, for Muhammad had
emerged out of a difficult historical period as one of the world's most
important and admired figures. Wolf saw in Muhammad a religious and
social reformer who became the epitome of the nonviolent
revolutionary. He found in Muhammad an Oriental Other whose
message had relevance for, and even solutions to, the identity crises that
Jewish and non-Jewish Germans Wolf were facing. Wolf felt
strengthened by the lessons he was learning from the Prophet's life, but
lamented that the war was making it too difficult for him to work
steadily on *Mohammed*. He wrote that the play was becoming too
powerful, and his awareness of this tortured him, because he was being
forced to fight a war in which he no longer believed. And he was
unable to easily do what had become important to him: to write a play
about his new hero, Muhammad. Wolf wrote that he felt the drama was
consuming him, turning his thoughts to

unserem Jahrhundert mit seinem blöden Wissensdünkel, dem Stolz auf das 120-km-Geschütz den Menschen in seiner alten Keuschheit und Reine entgegen-zustellen, [und] das Ringen einer Prophetenseele, die aus ähnlichem Wust und Wirrsal wie heute notgedrungen zuerst in das völlige Nichts geschleudert wird, um dann um so herrlicher und reiner zu Gott und dem Weltensinn sich zu erheben.[22]

(the twentieth century's stupid, conceited ignorance, its pride in long-distance artillery which served against the people in their ancient chastity and purity, [and] the struggles of a prophet's soul which, in similar confusion and chaos, is of necessity first flung into the absolute void in order to come more magnificently and purely back to God and to rise up and make sense of the world.)

Muhammad became for Wolf not only an example to emulate, but also a mouthpiece for his own emerging opinions about the meaning of social justice and the purpose of life.

Was Wolf only attracted to this Oriental because he believed Muhammad represented a completely new perspective, or is it possible that Wolf culturally identified with Muhammad? In other words, did the fact that Wolf was a Jewish-German writing during a time of debates about Jews as Orientals affect his decision to write a play about Muhammad? When Wolf was a university student, representations of Jews as Orientals were prevalent in such Jewish-German student publications as the popular *Blau-Weiß Blätter* (Blue-White Newsletters), with which he would have come into frequent contact.[23] Furthermore, *Mohammed* was written after the appearance of Jakob Wassermann's essay "Der Literat oder Mythos und Persönlichkeit," was completed the same year as Wassermann's "Der Jude als Orientale," and was revised following Krojanker's collection of essays entitled *Juden in der deutschen Literatur*. In fact, Wassermann's description of Jews in "Der Jude als Orientale" reflects concerns about the issues of character similar to those that Wolf dwelt on in *Mohammed*. Whereas Wassermann finds certain positive attributes representative for the Oriental Jew, Wolf ascribed these same characteristics to Muhammad: he is godly, lonely, radical, and prophetic. Muhammad thus seems to have symbolized for Wolf both a foreign solution to contemporary German problems *and* the vindication of an Oriental — and thus Jewish — perspective with which he, as a Jewish-German, could identify.

A critic with Wassermann's point of view could argue that Wolf, by presenting Muhammad's teachings to German society in order to foster a respect for Eastern culture, had fulfilled his role as a Jewish-German artist. While Wolf praised Muhammad the Oriental to a Western audience, he also illustrated the Prophet's importance to his own Jewish-German background. In many references to his play, Wolf emphasized the connections between the Islamic and Jewish religions. For example, in a rush of enthusiasm after reading the Qur'an, he wrote to his mother

that the "crowning verse" of the Qur'an ("God — there is no other God
than He, the living one, the constant one") is a paraphrase of the
"Schema Isroel." He added that the story of how Ibrahim (Abraham) had
a dialogue with the sun, moon, and stars, and was the first to worship
only one Lord, far surpasses the Old Testament in form and clarity.[24]
Wolf was so taken with this verse from the Qur'an that he incorporated
it into his drama: in the hope that Muhammad will be converted to
monotheism, Waraka reveals to Muhammad the story of how Abraham
became convinced of the singularity of God (I.24).

Wolf makes frequent references to the Hebrew Bible throughout
Mohammed. When Bahirah recognizes Muhammad as God's prophet,
he tells Muhammad, "Lege deine Hand auf mein Haupt . . . und sprich:
Ich bin der Löwe von Ismaels Stamm, der Gesippe Judas, Davids
Wurzel, aufzutuen das Buch und zu brechen die sieben Siegel" (Lay
your hand on my head . . . and say: I am the lion from Ismael's tribe,
Judah's clan, David's roots, here to open the book and break the seven
seals) (14); Bahirah thereby directly connects Muhammad to the heroes
of the Hebrew Bible. The pilgrims from Medina, initially wondering
whether Muhammad is really a prophet of God, ask if he can do what
the Jews praise their fiery prophets for (IV.61). After they become
convinced that he is indeed God's prophet, they proclaim him the voice
of the envoy who destroyed the golden calf (IV.69), thereby figuratively
tracing Muhammad's lineage back to Moses. To be sure, Wolf was being
true to the traditional sources in having Bahirah and the pilgrims from
Medina make these connections. The Arabian peninsula had large
Jewish and Christian populations, and the Muslims understood Muhammad to be one in the long line of Judeo-Christian prophets. However,
Wolf did not need to emphasize these points or make numerous,
specific references to the Hebrew Bible in telling Muhammad's story.
That he did so at all is significant: he was revealing the connections
Muslims made between their faith and his.

Wolf depicted Mecca as a place where not only the political and
social systems were dysfunctional, but where religion had also become
corrupt. Worship of the gods had become self-serving and shallow —
little more than a way of insuring success in business. Recognition of
and respect for the gods from the other clans would guarantee
diplomatic relations; as long as all the gods were regarded as equals,
then all the tribes could be equal partners in trade. In order to show the
amount of pressure this cultural mandate placed on Muhammad, Wolf
incorporated the "Satanic Verses" into his drama. It is crucial to the
leaders of Mecca that Muhammad renounce his claim that there is only
one God, and proclaim Him instead to be merely one among others;
they do not care what Muhammad really believes, just that he make this
diplomatic gesture to keep the peace (IV.62). Under much duress,
Muhammad agrees to make a public pronouncement that his God is an

equal among those of all the clans. El Walid, one of the powerful tribal leaders, bluntly expresses what this gesture will mean for Mecca: when Muhammad recognizes his people and his people's gods anew, Meccans will be able to revive commerce, join hands again, and enjoy peace, harmony, happiness, and material well-being (IV.62–3). Muhammad supposedly agrees to stop teaching about his God. Even the members of Muhammad's clan are thrilled with the Prophet's decision to capitulate to these demands, because it will restore good tribal relations. Muhammad's uncle, Abu Talib, congratulates him for being reasonable. He reassures Muhammad that he is doing the right thing in upholding his people's traditional understanding of religion. The best man is one who is deeply indebted to his people, Abu Talib reminds him (IV.63).

Nevertheless, Muhammad cannot go through with it. Unlike that of the other leaders, his faith is real, and he cannot compromise it:

> Was steht ihr gaffend? Wunderts euch? Wollt ihr ein Schauspiel? Wollt sehen, wie ein Mensch von seinem Gotte fällt, wie Flammen prasseln um ein zuckend Herz und sprechen: wohl uns? — Weh euch! weh euch und euren kalten, sichern, harten Herzen, die nicht mehr bluten, nicht mehr gluten [sic] wollen! Was seht ihr bei dem Schein und steht auf sichrem Stein? Blind steht ihr, blutlos! (IV.64)

> (Why are you standing there gaping? Is it surprising? Do you want a drama? Like flames crackling around a fluttering heart, you want to see how a person falls away from his God, and you say: who, us? — Woe to you! woe to you and your cold, confident, hard hearts that can no longer bleed and no longer want to glow! What do you see in the light while you stand on solid ground? You stand there blind and bloodless!)

He tells them that he cannot remain quiet when his soul is on fire about the truth that has been revealed to him by God (IV.65). Muhammad announces to the Meccans that their tribal religions reflect their own shallowness and are, therefore, mere social constructions (IV.65). He declares that if they really want to find God they must smash the idols and listen for Him in their hearts (IV.66). He explains to his uncle that he has no choice but to break with tradition and family and follow his own religious convictions: the bonds of a people run deep, but more important are the call of God and his service to Him (IV.70).

In this scene Wolf rejected the notion that one should refrain from challenging one's religious traditions just to keep peace in the community. He also rejected the notion that religious beliefs can provide easy solutions to the complex questions of human existence. Understanding God is an intense, personal experience, requiring patience and courage. Simply accepting contrived answers from one's community of faith leads one astray, while being smug about one's religion — because questioning its tenets might produce turmoil — is equally misguided.

In the same scene Muhammad not only charges the Meccans to rethink their worldviews, but Wolf also directly challenged his audience, while watching his play, to reexamine their presuppositions about their religious beliefs. He anticipated a desire in the European audience to see Muhammad proved a fraud; for this, they are chastised ("Why are you standing there gaping? Is it surprising? Do you want a drama? . . . you want to see how a person falls away from his God, and you say: who, us? — Woe to you!"). He also accused the audience of blindly following their religions and of being as intolerant as the Meccans; Europeans have grown cold, dispassionate, and heartless because they have no real religious convictions ("woe to you and your cold, confident, hard hearts that can no longer bleed and no longer want to glow! What do you see in the light while you stand on solid ground? You stand there blind and bloodless!"). As Muhammad implores the Meccans to look into their hearts and find God, so did Wolf ask the same of his audience. Simultaneously, Wolf's plea is for Europeans — and especially Germans — to respect the genuine followers of other religions, including those of the Orient. In this way, Wolf addresses two German audiences at once. He asks the Jewish community to be tolerant of his independent exploration of religious beliefs, including those outside Jewish-German traditions, like Islam. Also, because he has made connections between Judaism and Islam — and, hence, between Jews and Orientals — Wolf asks the Christians in the audience to be tolerant of the Jews. Wolf is thereby able to secure a place for himself, albeit as a dissident, both within the Jewish community and within German culture as a whole.

Fighting in a senseless, gruesome war, Wolf encountered real questions about the nature of God and religion. By tracing Muhammad's struggles with his religious identity, Wolf himself was able to wrestle with answers to his own questions: what is the nature of revelation, God's plan and will, and the purpose of life? The difficulties Muhammad faces in the process of learning about God underscore the seriousness of Wolf's concerns. At first, Muhammad cannot make sense of God's communications. He confides to Chadidjeh, "Ich rede in Verwirrung, was ich nie gewußt; erhalte Antwort auf Fragen, die ich nie gestellt. Vielleicht ist's Wahn und Krankheit?" (I speak confusedly about what I have no knowledge, receive answers to questions I have never posed. Maybe this is all insanity and sickness?) (I.24). As he becomes more certain that it is indeed God who is directing his actions, he still wonders who God is and what humanity's purpose in the world is. When God finally reveals himself to Muhammad, it is through the written word, emblazoned in the sky above Mt. Hira (III.49).[25] Muhammad finally grasps the significance of God's disclosure of himself: there is no knowledge without revelation. The purpose of revelation is to give people access to God's will and, hence, His plan. Believers should have faith in God's plan and therefore open their hearts to Him no matter how disquieted His will may make them, concludes the Prophet (III.51).

Trusting God is not always comfortable for Muhammad, either. Just because Muhammad has faith in God and His plan does not mean he understands God's actions. Indeed, God seems to test Muhammad's faith throughout his ordeals. On Mt. Hira, God seems to strike Ali dead, and Muhammad cries out against it (III.52). Afterward, as a fight breaks out between the tribes, Muhammad wails again:

> O Herr, o Höchster, was tuest du mit deinem Menschen! Frieden wollt ich bringen und bring das Schwert! Dein Wort wollt ich entzünden und zünde Wahn! — Und doch ist es dein Wille! (III.57)

> (Oh Lord, oh one on high, what are you doing with your human creation? I wanted to bring peace, and instead I bring the sword! I wanted your word to ignite people, and instead I have set off mass insanity! — And yet it is your will!)

He struggles to balance his trust in God's plan — even if God wills turmoil and destruction — and his compassion for the fate of other human beings for whom he feels responsible (III.51–52). In other words, Muhammad comes to understand that he must listen to God in order to transform the world according to His will, and yet he cannot forget that his actions affect people's lives. For Muhammad, this is not just a personal, mental exercise: spiritual encounter must manifest itself as social action.

Muhammad's struggle mirrors Wolf's effort to have faith while friends (and others) died around him. By writing *Mohammed*, Wolf seemed to be looking for a revelation from God that would make sense of his senseless situation: God's revelation to Muhammad, after all, came in the form of the *written* word. Wolf, like Muhammad, needs to balance a trust that the awful things that happen are part of a larger plan with an attempt to prevent unnecessary suffering caused by oppression and violence. Muhammad resolves this conflict in part by taking courageous stands against those who would use religion for petty reasons or for personal gain. He teaches the Meccans that religion should help them become more ethical and socially committed people. He proclaims that life is about neither wars, plowshares, nor empire-building. It is about listening to one's heart. It is about every heart that rises up out of its own depths: people can become holy because they have the inherent ability to do so (II.39). Muhammad informs them further that understanding God's will can help them transcend the unimportant things in life:

> Sehet, ich reiße diese Binde fort von euren Augen, sehet nur, was war euer Leben, Sinnen, Trachten? Um Reichtum, Ehre, Land und hohes Alter, und alles Dinge, die vergehen! . . . Sehet, Euer Herz ist das größte Wunder! (IV.69–70)

(Look, I will rip these blindfolds from your eyes; see here, what were your lives, inclinations, endeavors? You strove for wealth, glory, land, and longevity — all things that pass! . . . Look, your heart is greater than them all!)

For Wolf, faith in God can be liberating, because it forces one to concentrate on changing both one's life and the social world for the better.

Muhammad comforts Wolf, because the Prophet assumes that — even if one does not understand the reasons why things happen in the world — there remains a purpose to life. Muhammad's life illustrates to Wolf that this purpose is to struggle to the best of one's ability to live a positive, meaningful life in this often incomprehensible world. At the end of the drama, Muhammad challenges people to risk their whole hearts in death as in life (IV.71). *Mohammed* ends with the Prophet's converts promising to take that risk (IV.71). Wolf, like Muhammad's converts, also spreads his message. Wolf's version of the Prophet's message transcended an understanding of Islam or Islamic history. He underscores a central idea, universal in scope. In the process of depicting Muhammad's message, Wolf clarified his own beliefs and challenged others to examine theirs.

Wolf needed to write *Mohammed* for several reasons. He needed to come to terms with his religious concerns and the cultural issues related to them; he wanted to base his rejection of the war upon the moral framework he had constructed from his resolution of these issues. He depicted Muhammad's tribulations and triumphs in order to teach both his readers and himself certain lessons. The lessons he learned from the figure of Muhammad include trusting one's heart to reveal God's plan and speaking the truth in the face of overwhelming danger. Most of all, Wolf learned from the figure of the Prophet to be courageous and to have hope. This knowledge allowed Wolf to criticize the war and, at the same time, to find religious meaning in it:

Gestern habe ich III,i des *Mohammed*, die Offenbarung auf dem Berge Hira, beendet. Die Front blitzte den Geist der Vernichtung hinein, meine Holzbude bebte gewiß nicht minder wie der Berg vor Mekka; aber ich durfte nach ehrlichem Ringen von jenem höchsten Wesen, das wir schauen sagen: " . . . Entweiche nicht, und ist dein Wille Wirbel und Vernichtung, *ich spüre deinen Willen auch im Bösen!*" Ich hoffe in Mohammed; Bein von meinem Bein und Fleisch von meinem Fleisch; ich habe mich selten so glücklich gefühlt wie hier draussen in meiner Einsamkeit (Bretterbude in einem verlassenen, verfallenen Infantriegraben) und gefunden, im Schaffen ist die einzige Bejahung des Lebens, weder im Genuß noch im vitalen Leben.[26]

(Yesterday I finished act III, scene 1 of *Mohammed*, the revelation on Mt. Hira. The front flashed with the specter of annihilation, and my wooden shack certainly shook no less than the mountain in front of Mecca. But after an honest struggle with the highest being we can behold, I was able to say: " . . . Do not run away; if you will turmoil and destruction, *I sense that it is your will even in this evil.*" I find hope in Muhammad; bone from my bone, and flesh from my flesh. I have rarely felt as fortunate as I do here, outdoors, in solitude (in a ramshackle hut in an abandoned, dilapidated infantry trench). And I have found that the only affirmation of life comes in creating, rather than in seeking pleasure or in leading a vigorous life.)

To Wolf's mind, Muhammad was no longer an exotic Other. Instead he became an *individual* — transcending ethnic, racial, and religious constraints — from whom Wolf learned a new perspective, thus helping him make some sense out of the crisis of meaning produced by the war. At the same time, he presented Muhammad as a relative, someone with whom Wolf could identify on a deeper level, because their personal histories were linked through their cultural and religious traditions. By identifying with Muhammad, Wolf could simultaneously affirm and criticize his cultural identities as a Jew and a German. Ultimately, it is not Muhammad's exoticism that Wolf found attractive; instead, Wolf praised those aspects of Muhammad's character and message that resonated universally. Indeed, this perspective is what makes Wolf's drama exceptional: unlike most German Orientalist literature from this period, *Mohammed* denied the dichotomies between West and East, emphasizing instead the similar issues — war, justice, faith — that all cultures face. In the process of developing the stance that one can recognize cultural differences while simultaneously identifying common ground, Wolf also found a way to accept and affirm his own Jewish-German identity.

Der Koran.

Aus dem Arabischen
übertragen und mit einer Einleitung versehen

Max Henning.

Leipzig

Druck und Verlag von Philipp Reclam jun.

*The translation of the Qur'an Wolf took with him
to the front during the First World War:
Max Henning's* Der Koran, *1901.*

5: "Bad" Orientals, "Good" Orientals, and Franz Werfel

WRITTEN ON THE eve of Nazi political victory in parliament, Franz Werfel's novel *Die vierzig Tage des Musa Dagh* (The Forty Days of Musa Dagh, 1933) retells the history of the pogroms by the Ottoman Turks against the Armenian peoples of Western Asia. By recounting this history in 1932–33, Werfel seems to draw prophetic parallels between Turkish policy and actions against the Armenians and Nazi policy and actions against the Jews, suggests Oskar Metzler (337). However, Werfel's depiction of Orientals is complex: such a simplistic reading is challenged by an analysis of Werfel's constructions of cultural difference.

Like Friedrich Wolf's *Mohammed: Ein Oratorium*, Werfel's novel criticizes materialism and imperialism, calling instead for religious renewal and positive community action as antidotes against them. Also like Wolf's drama, *Musa Dagh* recounts a historical event from the Orient that has relevance to the author's own position as a German-speaking Jew in Europe. Just as it was for Wolf, it was extremely important for Werfel to research the event he was depicting as thoroughly as possible. As a result, much is made of the historical accuracy of Werfel's account of the Armenian genocide, prompting Norbert Abels to proclaim that this work sticks to the facts more than any other historical novel of the twentieth century (94).

The style of Werfel's great epic of the Armenian struggle is rather predictable, as are many of its themes. Like *Mohammed*, *Musa Dagh*'s themes and style owe much to the legacy of literary expressionism. Although Walter Sokel argues that Werfel's involvement with literary expressionism ended in 1923, *Musa Dagh*'s themes of revolt, father-son conflict, and messianic social communion — not to mention the pathos and urgency of its style — indicate Werfel's continued connection with the genre.[1] At the same time, the personal struggles of the Armenian protagonist Gabriel reflect the identity concerns of Werfel as a Jewish-German author. His is that central experience of being split in two that also is foreordained in Jewish individuals and peoples by their ancient Jewish fate, notes Rudolf Kayser (26). From being ruptured to becoming unified, from being torn apart to becoming whole: the longing and the ordeal stem from centuries of Jewish existence in Europe — and these sentiments found their particular, contemporary expression in Werfel's literature.

Werfel was born into a prosperous, Jewish-German family in Prague but had a very close relationship with his Catholic, Czech nanny.[2] Although his family prided itself on being assimilated, Werfel was nonetheless taken to the synagogue on high holy days and was bar mitzvahed. At the same time, his nanny took him to mass every Sunday and impressed upon him that Jews should not mock the cross. According to Gunther Grimm, Prague was a very tense place for both non-Jewish and Jewish-Germans around the turn of the century because all Germans were regarded with resentment by the Czech people, over whom the Austro-Hungarian Empire ruled (260). At the same time, asserts Lionel Steiman, since the Christian Germans based their German nationalism on racial exclusiveness, Jewish-Germans also were regarded with suspicion by their compatriots (10). Therefore, Werfel's early identity was shaped by a sense of not fitting in anywhere: he was a Jewish child attracted to Catholicism, a member of a hated minority of Germans, who still was not necessarily considered "really" German because he was a Jew.

This feeling of alienation grew as Werfel matured. He moved to Germany and then to Austria, where he was deemed an outsider. Although he considered himself a bohemian and socialist of sorts, he married the wealthy and conservative socialite Alma Mahler; their relationship was further complicated by the fact that she was, by all accounts, openly anti-Semitic. In fact, Werfel had to officially quit the Jewish faith before she would agree to marry him.[3] And even though most of his friends were Jewish-Germans from literary circles, Werfel increasingly presented himself as a Christian writer and found fault with Zionist ideology. In 1916 he published "Die christliche Sendung" (The Christian Message), in which he publicly proclaimed himself a Christian author. After this, notes Peter Jungk, his friend Martin Buber spent a week trying to bring him back to the fold of Judaism. Werfel then reassured Buber that his identification with being a Jew was completely nationalistic although he vehemently opposed the ideas of particular Zionists of Prague (48–49). Rebelling against the fashion of identifying with the Jews of Eastern Europe that was prevalent among some of his intellectual friends, Werfel admitted that he felt nothing in common with them. Werfel disliked the Oriental Jews; his favorite childhood literature had been the novels of Karl May, and he had identified instead with May's fictional Orientals.[4] He proclaimed himself an assimilated, Christian, German-speaking Jew and was preoccupied with being accepted as all these things at once.

What brought these issues to a head were the two trips Werfel and Mahler took to North Africa and the Levant in 1925 and 1929. Here Werfel had to confront his attitudes toward the Jews, and toward Orientals in general. At first he could not understand why European Jews would want to live in Palestine: why would such a civilized people want to live such a primitive lifestyle? he asked. He was also distressed by the zeal of the Zionists, who he felt were repeating the mistakes of the patriotic European citizens they had despised for their pronounced nationalism. He lamented that the Jews of Europe, whom he considered to be so advanced, now felt they had to prove that they could do the same things they had scorned and had made fun of in other peoples (Werfel, "ÄT" 706). And yet Mahler's anti-Semitism contributed to making Werfel feel that he must defend the Zionists (Werfel, "ÄT" 739); by his next trip to Palestine, he had become genuinely appreciative of all the Zionists had accomplished there.

His attitude toward the entire region was mixed. He found the exotic landscape inspiring. But he also considered the Muslims to be fanatical — although he actually knew very little about Islam (Werfel, "ÄT" 714–15). Werfel's ignorance about Islam is evident in many passages in his "Ägyptisches Tagebuch" (Egyptian Diary), in which he reveals that he merely accepted centuries-old German negative stereotypes about the religion. He wrote that the supposed tragedy of Islam seemed to be that it had not undergone any theological development; it still corresponded to the world of the crusades, during which time its spiritual progress must have died out. Where are its mystical epochs, Werfel asked, its periods of internal struggle? A single schism split it in two, that of the Shi'as, he claimed. He concluded that Islam epitomized the horrors of a spiritual or secular realm that has gone into decline because it lacked an opposition — that revolutionary dissolution without which the cycle of a life is unthinkable (Werfel, "ÄT" 734–35). Ironically, the one type of Islam he found positive was Sufism, which has often been at the center of spiritual and political reform movements in the Islamic world. He was quite taken with Sufis, whom he described in his diary and novel as holy and noble.

Nevertheless, in the wake of the Arab massacres of Jewish settlers in Palestine in 1929, Werfel's respect for and sympathy with the goals of Jewish nationalism grew; he became convinced that the Jews would need to arm themselves in preparedness against future pogroms by the Arabs. And yet his major sympathies lay with those Jewish organizations that worked to establish peace with the Arabs through nonviolent means. His perception of Muslims was further complicated by his encounter with Armenian refugees in Damascus in 1929, where he heard first-hand accounts of their tragic history under the regime of the Young Turks. It was from this experience that he decided to write a novel about the Armenians' plight.

The plot of Werfel's very lengthy *Musa Dagh* is simple: Gabriel Bagradian is a forty-year-old Armenian who has been living in France for twenty-three years. He has a French wife (Juliette), a son (Stephan) whom they have raised French, and mostly French friends. Upon learning that he needs to take over the family business, he packs up his immediate family and heads for home in Ottoman-ruled Syria. There he learns that World War I has broken out, and that the Turks have begun a pogrom against the Armenians. According to the novel, Ittihad (the Young Turks' Party) is using the Armenians as scapegoats for their problems, and has begun deporting or exterminating them under the cloak of nationalism. The leader of the Young Turks, Enver Pasha, ignores protests from representatives of both their German allies (Pastor Johannes Lepsius) and of Turkish dervish orders (Agha Rifaat Bereket). With no hope of help in sight, Gabriel organizes a plan of resistance for the Armenians in his region. The Armenians set up camp on the mountain of Musa Dagh and manage to hold out against the Turkish army until they are finally saved by French warships. By the conclusion, both Gabriel and Stephan are dead, and Juliette is both mentally and physically ill. Yet Gabriel had found meaning for his life and became a hero to his people.[5]

That the Orient is both repulsive and attractive to Werfel is revealed in his characterization of the people in *Musa Dagh*. Werfel constructs a hierarchy of Otherness based upon his categorization of certain human qualities as inherently Eastern or Western; this pigeonholing determines the place of each character in the structure. Werfel seems to advocate the assimilation of Oriental culture into Western culture by making the most positively depicted character an assimilated Oriental. Gabriel combines an inherently Oriental, spiritual passion for his people with a Western-trained rationality:

> Er, der Pariser, Juliettens Gatte, der Gelehrte, der Offizier, der die Wirklichkeit des modernen Krieges kennt . . . er ist zugleich der Knabe, der sich mit uraltem Bluthaß auf den Erzfeind seiner Rasse [den Türken] wirft. Die Träume jedes Armenierjungen. (24)

> (He, the Parisian, Juliette's husband, the academic, the military officer who knows the realities of modern warfare . . . he is also the boy who, with an ancient ancestral hatred, throws himself on the archenemy of his race [the Turks]. The dreams of every Armenian boy.)

Because Gabriel possesses the best qualities of Eastern and Western cultures, he is the hero of the novel and becomes the savior of his people.

However, the perfect integration of these characteristics does not come easily for Gabriel. Throughout the novel, he struggles to overcome the alienation he experiences as someone who does not seem to belong anywhere. He longs to feel he is a member of a community and yet encounters problems in doing so. In his quest for social identity, Gabriel continually weighs the advantages and disadvantages of revitalizing his ties to Armenian culture or rejecting that culture in favor of the Western ways he had adopted. For example, in an attempt to heighten Gabriel's internal conflicts, the narrator refers to him as "the Parisian" even as the hero believes he is becoming increasingly Armenian. In addition, as James Davidheiser observes, the narrator constantly underscores Gabriel's tenuous position by referring to him as a foreigner among both the French and the Armenians (62–63). Throughout, Gabriel contends with what he perceives to be the opposing Oriental and European traits he possesses. Indeed, claims Davidheiser, the hero of Musa Dagh "is mainly in combat with the two cultures within his own self"; therefore, "the search for cultural and national identity in Bagradian is Werfel's poetic complement to the Armenian-Turkish struggle" described by the novel (61, 63). Gabriel depicts the two cultures represented within himself as being in conflict: his European self is frustrated with Orientals. He resents the fact that he is constantly reminded of his bond to them: "Jesus Christus, konnte man denn nicht ein Mensch an sich sein? Frei von diesem schmutzigen feindlichen Gewimmel . . . ?" (Jesus Christ! Could not one just be an individual, free from this filthy, hostile swarm?) (40). He considers himself above their petty squabbles (17), finds he cannot understand them (57), gets angry with their seeming passivity (97), and is often disappointed by their inability to measure up to his standards (240). He also privileges the needs of Europeans, like those of his wife Juliette, over those of the Armenians (369). In sum, he experiences a deep ambivalence about his connection to an Oriental people whom he has come to regard as inferior:

> Armenier! Uraltes Blut, uraltes Volk war in ihm. Warum aber sprachen seine Gedanken öfter französisch als armenisch, wie zum Beispiel jetzt? . . . Blut und Volk! . . . Geldwechsler, Teppichhändler, Juweliere. Dies also waren seine Brüder? Diese verschlagenen Gesichter, diese irisierenden Augen, die auf Kundschaft lauerten? Nein, für diese Bruderschaft dankte er, alles in ihm wehrte sich dagegen . . . . Er ging, mit Widerwillen geschüttelt, weiter. (40)

> (Armenian! An ancient blood-line surged in him. But why were his thoughts more often expressed in French than Armenian — like now, for example? . . . blood and folk . . . money-changers, carpet-sellers, jewelers. So these were his brothers? These beaten faces, these dilated eyes, furtively glancing about for customers? No thanks, he rejected such a brotherhood — everything in him was repelled by it . . . . He left, shaken with repugnance.)

It does not surprise him, then, that he must assume the role of leader among the Armenians; the "superiority" of his education and Western experience make him the only one qualified for it (256).

He admits that part of the reason for his alienation from his people stems from the fact that he already saw many things through Juliette's eyes (40). And yet, returning to his homeland has filled him with awe as he remembers how ancient and Biblical it is (20). Learning about the Turks' plans for the Armenians makes him feel guilty about his negative sentiments toward his people: "Peinliche Scham! Er, der noch vor kurzer Zeit mit Blicken des Widerwillens an den armenischen Händlern des Bazars vorübergegangen war, fühlte sich nun verantwortlich und in das Schicksal dieses Volkes hineinverwickelt" (Embarrassing shame. He, who a short time ago had looked at the Armenian merchants in the bazaar with repugnance, felt himself now responsible for, and caught up in, the fate of his people) (43). As he explores his Orientalness, Gabriel discovers that his many years in Europe had repressed Asia's force in his soul, but not smothered it (273). He grows to resent his French wife's haughty attitude toward the Armenians (268), and he finally rejects her for Iskuhi, who — because she is an Armenian — has a more ancient claim on him (827–28). By the end of the novel, Gabriel has come to the conclusion that he has found his identity by having linked himself to the fate of his people (973). As a final act, he chooses an Armenian death over a French life.

Werfel attributes different characteristics to the various Orientals in *Musa Dagh*. The Armenians living in Syria are characterized by Werfel as "good" Orientals: they are well-meaning, lovable, dependable, and estimable people (22), but somewhat naive and irrational. For example, unlike European children, Oriental children forgot their plans before they could execute them; they were carried along by short-sighted schemes and crudely instinctive urges (407). Nonetheless, the fact that they are a naturally sensitive, skilled, industrious, civilized "Intellektrasse" (race of intellectuals) (397) is repeated throughout the novel. Still their intellectuals are clearly unsophisticated compared with Europeans; the apothecary Krikor, one of the most learned men on Musa Dagh, had to make do with a scanty, Armenian store of knowledge (69). Because the Armenians understand this, their attitude toward Westerners is somewhat subservient. Feeling unworthy of Gabriel's love, Iskuhi reflects:

> Was war sie, was war Aram [ihr Bruder], was waren all die andern für nichtige Fliege gegen ihn? Rohe, schmutzige Bauern, ohne Gedanken im Kopf, ohne Gefühle im Herzen, die nicht ahnten, wer zu ihnen herabgestiegen war . . . . Was konnte sie leisten und opfern, um Gabriels würdig zu sein? Nichts! (755)

> (What was she, was Aram [her brother], were all the others, except insignificant fleas compared to him? Crude, dirty peasants, without thoughts in their heads, without feelings in their hearts, unable to comprehend who it was who had climbed down to be with them . . . . What could she achieve or sacrifice to make herself worthy of Gabriel? Nothing!)

The Armenians idolize Gabriel, recognizing his superiority, even if they sometimes resent or envy him for it. As their commander, they obey him, respect him, and are even grateful to him (729). Yet what arouses their ire is the disciplined relentlessness, the "European" in Gabriel's speech; because of this they cannot entirely accept him as one of their own (261).

When Gabriel decides it is important for his son to learn all he can about his heritage (193), his teachers make Stephan a true Armenian (196). The descriptions of Stephan's transformation from a European to an Oriental reflect some of Werfel's own prejudices toward Oriental culture. Gabriel notices that his son, since he began attending the Armenian school, had lost his European manners with amazing speed (219–20). Indeed, the more Oriental Stephan becomes, the less civilized he becomes. He grows wild and his fine French cultivation and learning falls away until it was as though he had never known civilized life (405–6). And yet the Armenian children cannot quite accept Stephan either, because his European traits set him off as different from them. Despite his attempts to revert entirely "ins Primitive" (to a primitive state) Stephan cares about keeping himself clean, successfully comes up with and executes plans, rejects superstition and mystical experience, and demonstrates the ability to lead (406–8). In many ways, he still represents the opposite of how Werfel characterizes his Armenian counterparts.

That Werfel prefers Armenian Orientals over Turkish ones manifests itself in their comparisons in *Musa Dagh*. Unlike the other Orientals in the region, Armenians are respectable people; the Armenians, as opposed to the Arabs and the other Eastern rabble-rousers, are quiet and reserved in public (100) and their villages are tidy and not to be compared with the wretched settlements of the Turks (56). Whereas the Armenians are smart and hard-working — and therefore successful in commerce, agriculture, and industry — the Turks are lazier and less intelligent (163–64). And Armenian women, unlike Muslim women, are pure and modest (613). Werfel's preference for Armenian Oriental culture over that of other Orientals is even apparent in his description of the landscape: he goes so far as to claim that the honey made in the Christian Armenian region tastes better, because their land is blessed; the Muslim regions, on the other hand, make the bees sick (55–56).

Indeed, the Turks represent the "bad" Orientals: they are barbaric, ignorant, and brutal, destroying the cultures they colonize. Words associated with filth, laziness, deception, and greed are constantly used to describe Turks. For example, the office of a Turkish bureaucrat is depicted in terms which elicit disgust: "Ein säuerlicher Juchtengeruch von Schweiß, kaltem Tabak, Trägheit und Elend erfüllte den Raum" (A sour stench consisting of sweat, stale tobacco, lethargy, and misery filled the room) (33). Even seemingly friendly Turkish officials are slaves to their ambition (129) and can be bought off (141); they are therefore deemed untrustworthy. Turkish men behave in stereotypically abominable ways toward women: when they encounter Iskuhi on a deportation march, one Turk tries to purchase her for his harem (128) and others gang-rape her (129–30). Because of their supposedly naturally sensuous natures, Turks exhibit a ridiculous "Asian" obsession with being ostentatious (501), which leads them to shamelessly and repeatedly plunder the Armenian villages (297). Because they realize that they are of an inferior race and uncultivated (314–15), their hatred of Gabriel and the Armenians for their success in the world is emphasized. In general, Werfel's characterization of Turks contains the type of polarities used to describe Turkey's two great leaders, Enver and Jemal Pasha, who also happen to be brothers. These Turks are represented as either frivolous or brutish:

> Enver Pascha war aus dem leichtesten Stoff, Dschemal Pascha aus dem schwersten Stoff der Welt gebildet. War an jenem alles träumerisch launenhaft, so an diesem alles leidenschaftlichen wüst. (501)

> (Enver Pasha was made of the lightest material, Jemal Pasha of the heaviest. If the one consisted entirely of dreamy capriciousness, the other consisted of impassioned desolation.)

Their religion, Islam, appears to reinforce the negative traits in the Turks.[6] That Islam does not teach the Turks to be pious is illustrated by the fact that they spend their Fridays looking for mosques *and* "Weiber und Lustbarkeit" (broads and amusements) (323). In fact, the Muslims are associated with having loose sexual morals (741). Furthermore, their religious convictions do not run deep. Clearly, it is dangerous for the Armenians that they are forced to live next to Muslims (336). After plundering Gabriel's village,

> reich gewordene Araber und Türken verbrüderten sich. Niemals hatten sie schönere Häuser gesehen . . . . Aus den Kirchen hatte man in Handumdrehen Moscheen gemacht. Schon am ersten Abend fand ein Gottesdienst statt. Die Mollahs dankten Gott für den neuen herrlichen Besitz, den freilich noch ein Schatten trübe, das freche Leben der unreinen Christenschweine dort oben auf dem Berg. Es sei die Pflicht jedes Gläubigen, sie zu vertilgen. Dann erst würde man sich des üppigen Gütes in gerechter Frömmigkeit erfreuen dürfen. Die Männer verließen mit funkelnden Augen die Moscheen. (507)

> (Arabs and Turks, grown rich, swore eternal friendship to one another. Never before had they seen more beautiful houses . . . . In the twinkling of an eye, the church had been converted into a mosque. They held services in it that very evening. The mullahs thanked God for their new, wonderful possessions — even though they still carried with them the reminder of those filthy Christian dogs up there on the mountain. It was the duty of every believer to exterminate them. Only then would one be allowed to enjoy these lavish goods with a justified sense of piety. The men left the mosque with flashing eyes.)

Their religion allows the Muslims to justify the barbarous acts they commit.

Yet Werfel did not want to paint an entirely manichean depiction of Turks and Armenians. Upon perusal of a draft of his novel, he realized he had done precisely this. Do not polemicize against the Turks, Werfel wrote to himself in the manuscript's margins; so notes Jungk (143). He tried to keep in mind that he needed to show that there were "good" Turks, including those who disagreed with the policies of Ittihad. As a soldier himself, Werfel may have actually met and trained with Turkish troops, some of whom were stationed in Austria during the first World War. Hence Gabriel admits there are some virtuous people among the Turks: in the war he had come to know the patience and kindness of their poor. "Sie sind nicht schuld" (they are not to blame), says Gabriel (82). Werfel claimed that it was the Turkish middle class who supported the Young Turks, not the peasants (180). Indeed, "Hunderte von gutherzigen Türken rings im Land, denen das unmenschliche Elend der Deportierten [Armenier] das Herz zerbrochen hatte" (hundreds of good-hearted Turks across the land, whose hearts were broken by the plight of the [Armenian] deportees), risked their lives to try to help them (705). And yet most of these same peasants are still repeatedly characterized rather negatively. In an attempt to find something else he can praise Turks for, Werfel emphasized that Turks — and especially Anatolians — were famous soldiers (388). This nevertheless functions as a backhanded compliment. Whereas the Armenians are an "Intellektrasse" (race of intellectuals), the Turks are a "Militärrasse" (military race) (397); the one group has brains whereas the other has only brawn. In fact, the Turkish sense of self-worth is so bound up with military conquests that Gabriel believes if the Armenians can defeat them just once, they will humble the Turks to the extent that they will never be able to recover from it (278). Even Turks who possess seemingly positive traits are somehow suspect, if not simply inferior, Orientals.

Just as Orientals are divided into two groups — the "good" and the "bad" — Europeans also come in two varieties. The first group is suspicious of Eastern culture and therefore ethnocentric. For example, Juliette constantly refers to Orientals as primitives. She claims that the Armenians may be an ancient people, but they are not a "Kulturvolk" (people of culture) like the French (210). Because of this, she believes that her suffering on Musa Dagh is more significant than that of the others (377). Nevertheless, Juliette is surprised to learn that, even though Iskuhi is an Armenian woman, she is both beautiful and educated; in order to make sense of it, Juliette reasons that Iskuhi cannot really be Armenian:

> Weißt du, daß ich im Grunde die Orientalinnen mit ihrer Faulheit und
> ihren schlaffen Bewegungen alle verabscheue . . . . Aber du bist ja gar

keine Orientalin, Iskuhi. Wenn du so gegen das Licht sitzt, hast du
ganz blaue Augen . . . . (208)

(Do you know, that, in principle, I abhor all Oriental women, with
their laziness and their floppiness . . . . But you're not an Oriental
woman at all, Iskuhi. When you sit against the light like that, your eyes
are quite blue.)

Likewise, the American Gonzague Maris is amazed to find in the
wretched Orient a village as beautiful and as full of civilized people as
Gabriel's (73). And yet, he cannot fully empathize with their plight,
because they are clearly an inferior people: "Diesen Armeniern ist nicht
zu helfen, denn sie sind und bleiben feierliche Narren" (These
Armenians cannot be helped because they are, and will remain, absolute
fools) (313). He sees his role among them in setting a good example:
from him perhaps the Armenians could learn to be more refined (373–
74). Although Werfel did not paint these Europeans in the best light, he
established empathy for their difficult situation as foreigners caught in
the struggles between Armenians and Turks, even as he criticized their
intolerance: they are by no means the villains of the story.

The second group of Europeans may not really understand Oriental
culture, but they nevertheless prove that they can have empathy for the
Armenians. Indeed, they strive to be the moral saviors of the latter. The
German pastor, Johannes Lepsius, intervenes three times on behalf of
the Armenians: he speaks with the Turkish government, the German
government, and an order of Turkish Sufis. Although his mission fails,
his pleas on behalf of the Armenians are passionate. Lepsius argues that,
because he is German, he cares about the sufferings of ethnic minorities;
after all, the Germans are in the minority in Europe (646). He admits that
he knows nothing about Islam — except that it is the fanatic enemy of
Christianity and, thus, of Armenians (654–55); still, his conscience pricks
him for his ignorance when Turkish Sufis reach out to him in friendship
and in the common cause of helping end the genocide (660). Similarly,
Werfel emphasized the compassion and sense of moral mission of the
French admiral who rescues the Armenians from Musa Dagh:

denn es bestehe kein Zweifel darüber, daß ein französischer Admiral
einen so tapferen Stamm des mißhandelten armenischen *Christenvolkes*
nicht einfach seinem Schicksal überlassen werde. (941, emphasis
added)

(There was no chance that a French admiral would leave such a brave
clan of mistreated Armenian *Christians* to its fate.)

Nonetheless both men seem to want to help the Armenians mostly
because they are a Christian people like them — and not just any
persecuted group. Even though Armenians are Orientals, Lepsius states

that he can identify with them, and therefore wants to help them, because they share the same faith (666).

By characterizing the people in his novel according to such a hierarchy of preference, Werfel reproduced stereotypical representations of Orientals constructed by German culture over a long period of history — constructions that favor Western culture over what he considered to be Eastern culture. Whereas Westerners are seen as rational, self-controlled, civilized, and progressive, Orientals are depicted as irrational, overly passionate, backward, and potentially dangerous. In his "Ägyptisches Tagebuch," Werfel summed up the supposed differences in the way Europeans and Orientals work: "Die europäische Arbeit ist gleichmäßig, statisch, zweckhaft, provident, die orientalische stoßweise, dynamisch, auf gut Glück, durch Ekstase getrieben" (European work is consistent, static, purposeful, providential; Oriental work is spasmodic, dynamic, and propelled by good luck and ecstasy) (709). He projected these assumed differences onto both cultures, and yet he identified himself in this respect as an Oriental type of worker (709).

The differences in the characters of Lepsius and Enver Pasha perfectly mirror these paradigms. The debate between them over the fate of the Armenians is as equally significant in establishing the "correct" and "incorrect" positions on this subject as it is in reinforcing the supposed differences between the two cultures. While Lepsius is the epitome of Western enlightenment and humanist ideals, Enver Pasha embodies stereotypical Oriental despotism and barbarism. On the subject of the Armenian deportations, Enver Pasha declares:

> Ich werde Ihnen eine Gegenfrage stellen, Herr Lepsius. Deutschland besitzt glücklicherweise keine oder nur wenig innere Feinde. Aber gesetzt den Fall, es besäße unter anderen Umständen innere Feinde, nehmen wir an Franco-Elsässer, Polen, Sozialdemokraten, Juden, und zwar in größerer Menge als das der Fall ist. Würden Sie da, Herr Lepsius, nicht jegliches Mittel gutheißen, um ihre schwerkämpfende, durch eine Welt von äußeren Feinden belagerte Nation vom inneren Feinde zu befreien? Würden Sie es dann auch so grausam finden, wenn man die für den Kriegsausgang gefährlichen Bevölkerungsteile einfach zusammenpackte und in entlegene, menschenleere Gebiete verschickte? (161)

> (I want to ask *you* a question, Mr. Lepsius. Luckily, Germany has no, or at least very few, internal enemies. But suppose, under different circumstances, it did have internal enemies — for instance, Franco-Alsatians, Poles, Social Democrats, Jews — and in greater numbers than is the case now. Mr. Lepsius, would not you use every means possible to free your fighting nation, which is surrounded by external enemies, from its internal enemies? Would you then find it so horrible, if one were to pack up and ship off to remote, uninhabited areas those elements of the population jeopardizing the outcome of the war?)

Pastor Lepsius's response is one of outrage:

> Johannes Lepsius muß sich mit beiden Händen anhalten, um nicht aufzuspringen und hervorzufuchteln: "Wenn die Regierenden meines Volkes," ruft er sehr laut, "ungerecht, gesetzlos, unmenschlich (unchristlich hat er schon auf der Zunge gehabt) gegen ihre Landsleute von anderem Stamm oder anderer Gesinnung vorgingen, so würde ich mich im selben Augenblick von Deutschland lossagen und nach Amerika ziehn!" (162)

> (Johannes Lepsius had to hold himself down with both hands, so as not to jump up and shake his fist wildly. "If the government of my people," he loudly proclaimed, "acted against its citizens of other ethnicities or other convictions in an unjust, lawless, inhumane ("unchristian" was also on the tip of his tongue) manner, then I would instantly dissociate myself from Germany and move to America!")

The Turk's reaction is predictably crude:

> Langer Augenaufschlag Enver Paschas: "Traurig für Deutschland, wenn andere auch so denken wie Sie. Ein Zeichen, daß Ihrem Volke die Kraft fehlt, seinen nationalen Willen rücksichtslos durchzusetzen." (162)

> (A long look from Enver Pascha: "Too bad for Germany, if others think like you. It is a sign that your people do not have the strength to assert their national will without consideration for others.")

Because Werfel was seemingly quite oblivious to the serious gains Nazis were making in Germany and Austria, it is bitterly ironic that he put these words in the Pasha's mouth. Little did Werfel know that he would soon be put in the real position of being declared an "internal enemy" whose choices were either to be rounded up or to leave for America.

Complicating his clear hierarchy of preference for Western culture over its Eastern counterpart, in *Musa Dagh* Werfel erected two other paradigms about the Orient. These paradigms, which reflect both admiration and disgust for the Orient, are typical of European Orientalist literature.[7] For instance, Werfel presents a pristine, idyllic Orient: it is a fanciful representation of the classical, Islamicate world. This ahistorical fantasy is filled with religious mystics, romantic scenery, flowery poetry, ancient traditions, and blissfully contented people; these Orientals are nonthreatening and are thus worthy of Werfel's respect. Gabriel's friend the Agha — who is an old-fashioned, mystical Turkish Sufi — serves as the embodiment of these values.

But Werfel also paints an entirely opposite view of the region: the historical Orient is a powerful and dangerous place. In this view, the Orientals adopt the worst traits of Western civilization, which causes them to become even more monstrous barbarians. In *Musa Dagh* this Westernization has made noble savages ignoble. Instead of treasuring the "old ways," Westernized Orientals are driven by materialism, nationalism, technology, and atheism. According to Werfel, where the Young Turks have erred is in trying to be "modern" — a condition he equated with being secular and progressive. Although Werfel did not necessarily criticize the West for having modern values, he did condemn the Orientals who brought such ideas to the East.

Werfel asserts as much by way of a conversation in the novel between Turkish Sufis and Lepsius. During the course of the dialogue, Lepsius and the Sufis come to understand that the Armenians — who have served as a conduit between East and West for years — are partially to blame for their own persecution. Werfel argues that the Europeans are ultimately to blame for the ascendancy of Ittihad; for their own material and political gain, the Europeans brought "progress" to the region, using the Armenians as their intermediaries. One of the Sufis complains to Lepsius about the Europeans' colonization and the Armenians' role in it:

> ihr Europäer [habt] euch in das innere Leben des Reiches gemengt, habt Reformen gefordert und uns für billiges Geld Allah und den Glauben abkaufen wollen. Die Armenier aber waren eure Geschäftsreisenden. (663)

> (you Europeans meddled with the interior life of the empire, demanded reform, and wanted to buy up our faith in exchange for cheap money. But the Armenians were your traveling salesmen.)

To which Lepsius replies, "Und es ist ja selbstverständlich, daß sich die Armenier als das schwächere und tätigere Volk nach ihnen gesehnt haben" (And it is self-evident that the Armenians, as the weaker and more active people, yearned for these things) (663–64).

Thus, argues Werfel in this passage, the peoples of the East neglected their religion and culture, adopting instead what he considered to be Western values: the secularism, materialism, and nationalism that the Young Turks championed. Whereas all Islamic peoples had lived together in peace, and people of all religions lived in harmony with them, nationalism and Western values had torn the various peoples asunder. This is the reason for the pogroms against the Armenians, Werfel argues; they helped bring the destruction on themselves. If the Armenians had not encouraged the Turks to become more Western in their thinking, then the Turks would not have been able to persecute them so thoroughly — indeed, he suggests, the Turks might never have come up with the idea at all. However, the Sufis and Lepsius agree that the Turkish-Armenian collusion does not justify the persecutions of the Armenians (663–71).

Particularly shocking about Werfel's contention in the above passage of *Musa Dagh* is the fact that, although he repeatedly asserted in the novel his belief that the Armenians are an unjustly and universally oppressed people, he also accused them of having paved the way for their own colonization and genocide. The East is better off if left unsullied by the corrupting ideas of the West. Sadly, later statements Werfel made about the participation of the Jews in their own genocide echo the arguments he was making about the Armenians in his novel.[8]

The story told in Werfel's novel reveals the complex identity issues with which Werfel was struggling. Parallels do exist between the historical situations of the Armenians and Jewish-Germans like Werfel — and Werfel was not unaware of them. Metzler reveals that, just as the author found parallels between Armenian and Jewish histories, so too did he give the Armenian figures in his book — particularly the intellectuals — traits that correspond to his image of historical Jews; to reinforce the image, he used richly religious symbolism containing elements from the Old Testament's "Books of Moses" in his treatment of the events on Musa Dagh (the "Moses Mountain") (340). Other critics, like Jungk, have pointed out similar parallels,[9] as well as the fact that Werfel modeled many of the important Armenian characters after specific Jews he had known in Prague (142–43). Indeed, Werfel made the connections between these groups quite explicit in the novel. Like the Jews, "Armenier [zu] sein ist eine Unmöglichkeit" (it is impossible to be Armenian) (62) and "Armenieraugen sind fast immer groß, schreckensgroß von tausendjährigen Schmerz-Geschichten" (Armenian eyes are almost always too big, terrifyingly huge from thousands of years of suffering) (93); they are like the "Kindern Israel in der Wüste" (children of Israel in the desert) (327).

Clearly Werfel projects onto all of Jewry his understanding of history from a European Jewish perspective. The history of Sephardic Jewry differs markedly from that of European Jews: Sephardic experiences of living in Islamicate cultures have been largely positive. The Turks invited the Jews who had been expelled from Spain in 1492 to return to North Africa and Western Asia, from where they had originally come; thus the refugee Jews came to live in the Ottoman Empire and in other areas of the region alongside other Jews who had never left. Together the Jews became integral to the social and economic life of North Africa and Western Asia. However, the mainly negative experiences of Ashkenazic Jews living in Europe bring Werfel to project onto Muslims a very different interpretation of the history of their relations: a history of conflict rather than of relatively peaceful coexistence between Jews and Muslims.

Furthermore, Steiman suggests that Werfel did not have the precarious situation of Jewish-Germans in the early 1930s specifically in mind when he wrote *Musa Dagh*. After the Nazi period, both Werfel and his wife claimed the novel had been an unconscious projection of what was to come for German Jewry. Yet his original intention had been to accurately portray the Armenians and the world in which they lived in order to alert Europeans to their plight. Indeed, while he was occupied with writing his Armenian novel, Werfel failed to take serious notice of the rise to power of the Nazis. At the time he was reported to have predicted that the situation might get bad for the Jews under the Nazis, but that this would only be temporary — compared to what had happened to the Armenians, the world was in good shape (75). In fact, claims Jungk, Werfel told Alma that his impression of Hitler was not altogether bad; when the Nazis came to power, he swore an oath of loyalty to the regime, hoping that this would protect the future sales of *Musa Dagh*, with which he was much more preoccupied at the time than the plight of the Jews (139–40).

Werfel seemed to be working out his own, individual issues of identity through the character of Gabriel Bagradian, an assimilated Oriental living in Western society, married to a European woman. Gabriel experiences a sense of double alienation and strives to find a way to make sense of his life. He tells Juliette, "Wir gehören weniger dorthin, wo wir herkommen, als wo wir hinwollen!" (We belong less to where we are from than to where we want to go) (379). Later he tells Iskuhi, "Mein Lebtag habe ich immer das Fremde gesucht. Es hat mich verführt, doch niemals glücklich gemacht. Und auch ich habe das Fremde verführt und nicht glücklich gemacht" (My whole life I have sought out what was foreign to me. It seduced me, but never made me happy. And I have seduced it too, but I could not make it happy either) (732). He is in conflict about how he ultimately fits into the larger scheme of things — are his roots important or not? Gabriel finds the solution to his identity problems in an increasing awareness of the importance of spirituality: by gaining a mystical reunderstanding of his roots and the significance of belonging to a persecuted group, Gabriel finds meaning in his existence. Indeed, he inspires other members of the community through his example. By the end of the novel, Gabriel has come full circle, fulfilling a destiny about which he had prophetically fantasized as a child:

> Die wilden Phantome jedes Armenierjungen . . . . Der blutige Sultan Abdul Hamid hat einen Ferman wider die Christen erlassen. Die Hunde des Propheten, Türken, Kurden, Tscherkessen, sammeln sich um die grüne Fahne, um zu sengen, zu plündern und das Armeniervolk zu massakieren. Die Feinde aber haben nicht mit Gabriel Bagradian gerechnet. Er vereinigt die Seinen. Er führt sie ins Gebirge. Mit unbeschreiblichem Heldenmut wehrt er die Übermacht ab und schlägt sie zurück. (24)

> (The wild fantasies of every Armenian boy . . . . The bloody Sultan Abdul Hamid has issued a ferman against the Christians. The hounds of the Prophet — Turks, Kurds, Circassians — rally around the green banners to scorch, plunder, and massacre the Armenian people. But the enemies have not factored Gabriel Bagradian into their plans. He unites his people. He leads them into the mountains. With

indescribable heroism he fights off the superior forces and drives them back.)

However, Gabriel's understanding of himself and his Oriental heritage is, to a large extent, determined by his identification with a Western worldview — the same ideology that Werfel condemns for its influence on the Young Turks, which in turn leads to the destruction of the Armenians. Whereas Werfel and Gabriel see themselves as empathetic to the values and traditions of their minority groups, they do so through the filter of the perspective of a majority culture — in Werfel's case German, and in Gabriel's case generic Western. In fact, Gabriel's and Werfel's attitudes toward Armenians are often downright patronizing. While they are able to criticize Western culture for not being tolerant of Oriental culture, they often evaluate the Orient through distorted European constructs. After all, Gabriel is not just an Armenian, but a French Armenian; and Werfel is not simply a Jew, but a German and a Christian as well. In other words, although European Jews histori-cally have been the victims of anti-Semitic Orientalism, because Werfel's perceptions and attitudes were shaped by the West, he also adopted Orientalist attitudes toward the East. Werfel thus makes fun of a Swiss Armenian in his novel who falsely prophesies that the Armenians are not really in any danger living among the Turks because soon the sun of civilization will also rise over Turkey (67) — even while, as he was writing *Musa Dagh* in 1933, Werfel failed to grasp the magnitude of what he called the temporary setback that lay ahead for the Jews under Hitler. Werfel simply could not imagine that "his" German *Kulturvolk* could act as barbarically as the Turks. Ironically, this sentiment echoes the attitude of Juliette, whom Gabriel criticizes in the novel for being so narrow-minded.

In *Musa Dagh* Werfel projected onto the Orient what he considered the ills of Europe. Those foreign evils introduced by the Ittihad party — modernism, nationalism, the perversion of religion, and racism — are the very maladies Werfel had diagnosed in Europe. In fact, he delivered two lectures in several German-speaking cities during this time that emphasize the evils of materialism and the importance of spirituality. The first, entitled "Kunst und Gewissen" (Art and Conscience), argued that the path of blind glorification of technological progress, encouraged by the US and USSR, was leading Europe to a spiritual crisis. Werfel saw this as an underlying reason for the support of the Nazis in Germany. Jungk explains that, as far as Werfel was concerned, only recovering the miraculous in humanity could rescue it from global savagery: against this barbarism Werfel prescribed an uprising of spirituality (130). The second lecture, entitled "Kann die Menschheit ohne Religion leben?" (Can Humanity Live without Religion?), proclaimed that Catholicism repre-sented the true path to salvation in an age cursed by the twin evils of communism and Nazism. Lore Foltin suggests that, for Werfel, awakened spirituality was the only remedy for the empty secularism offered by these pernicious ideologies (73–74).

Werfel's notions about the function of a religious worldview — which he used to criticize Nazism — were similar to those shared by contemporaneous German *völkisch* thinkers. That Werfel espoused such a conservative *völkisch*ness in 1933 is astonishing, given that such ideologies were not only historically linked with anti-Semitism but also had become powerful weapons used by the Nazis against the Jews. Werfel's desire to be seen as spiritually advanced had made him blind to the potentially dangerous consequences of his ideas. He simply did not recognize that the religious worldview he championed along with *völkisch* thinkers was based not on an elevated form of spiritualism, but rather a perverted one.

Over a period of many years, Werfel had worked out for himself a spiritual understanding of the meaning of his life. His first trip to Palestine reawakened in him a sense of connection to the Jews. Later, interest in his Jewish heritage spurred him on to spend many months intensively studying Jewish history, sacred texts, and culture, as well as Hebrew. Despite this immersion in things Jewish, his studies did not make him more devoted to Judaism as he had wished, but instead strengthened him to spurn a more orthodox form of Judaism in favor of a Christian worldview. Marysia Turrian notes that he became critical of those Jews he regarded as obsessed by law, incapable of love, and lacking the courage to give up the Torah in exchange for the "Liebes-religion" (religion of love) they really long for: Christianity (90). According to George Buck, Werfel believed that Jews have an important role to play in the religious order of things: only through the testament of the Jew and his ceaseless persecution is the truth of Jesus Christ confirmed (94). The Jews who are able to integrate a secure sense of their Jewish heritage with an acceptance of the teachings of Christianity (especially Catholicism) have the best of both worlds.

Werfel did not argue that Jews should renounce their origins and convert to Catholicism.[10] Instead he struggled to integrate his adopted religious identity and his culturally determined religious identity. His wish to be seen both as fully assimilated into Christian German society and as someone with a unique position as a Jewish-German in that society is reflected throughout his writings. Echoing Wassermann, Werfel believed that the historical mission of Jews is to function as emissaries to the West for the mysticism of the East. Steiman notes that Werfel contended that most Jews who come to the West lose their spiritual equilibrium and become increasingly secular and materialistic (177). However, those Jews — like Werfel himself — who accept the historical truth of Christianity are able to regain their balance and understand the need for religiosity as an antidote to the ills of the West. In other words,

Christian Jews, like Werfel, find meaning in life as religious individuals who have come to accept their Oriental origins and Western dispositions, thereby integrating the best of both cultures. Like Gabriel, they have the special spirituality and insight to constructively make a difference in the world.

In keeping with Werfel's spiritual perspective, religiosity (practicing an allegiance to God) plays a determining factor in whether the characters in *Musa Dagh* are judged positively or negatively. Characters depicted as having strong religious convictions are considered morally superior people, regardless of their ethnicity. For example, pious Turkish Sufis and Muslim peasants are praised and are depicted as working to counteract the pogrom against the Armenians: the Agha is one of the most important spiritual forces in the novel, and the Turkish peasant who rescues Stephan is devoutly religious (718). At the same time, the Armenian priest from Musa Dagh (Ter Haigasun) provides the most insightful and ethical guidance to his people. And the two Europeans who risk the most to try to save the Armenians are the German pastor Lepsius and the staunchly Catholic French admiral. Being truly committed to God — and not just paying lip service to Him — makes one genuinely human and humane. Hence Gabriel, with whom Werfel identifies, proclaims, "Beten Sie . . . Aber man muß Gott auch unterstützen!" (Pray . . . But one must also support God!) (98).

Werfel characterized secularized people, especially secularized Turks, most negatively; in fact, he portrayed the members of the Ittihad party most critically. They have led their people away from Islam by adopting atheism and/or by perverting their religion for their own purposes. The Agha explains his dislike of them:

> Diese Verräter, diese Atheisten, die das Weltall Gottes vernichten, nur um selbst zu Macht und Geld zu kommen? Das sind keine Türken und keine Moslems, sondern nur leere Lästerer und Geldschnapper. (48)

> (These traitors, these atheists who would even annihilate God's universe in order to get power and money? They are neither Turks nor Muslims, but rather blasphemers and money-grabbers.)

Similarly, those Protestant Armenian pastors who care more about their personal reputations than listening to God, end up making choices that adversely affect many people; most of the Armenians who choose to wait with Pastor Aram Tomasian for deportation, instead of following Gabriel up the mountain, die horribly. Furthermore, thoroughly secularized Europeans, like Juliette and Maris, are less and less sympathetically portrayed, until they become some of the least respected members of the community on Musa Dagh. They become consumed with self-pity, feeling only bitterness about being stuck in the Orient instead of displaying a Christian sense of compassion toward the Armenians (442).

Werfel contended that the problem with the Young Turks was they selectively focused on only those parts of their history they could exploit for their political agenda, which latter had been shaped by foreign, secular forces. The Agha explains that the Young Turks thus emphasize a history of Turkish martial success, but downplay the Islamic tradition of tolerance for other cultures and religions; indeed, their newly adopted way of thinking excludes the Islamic tradition altogether (48). Even those Ittihad supporters who think they are religious are only practicing a distorted form of Islam, one that has been corrupted and manipulated by the nationalistic hatred on the part of the Young Turks (297). They have recklessly adopted Western "progress" without understanding it. The Agha proclaims that only those Turks who have remained firmly committed to authentic religiosity and cultural tradition — and have, therefore, rejected the policies of Ittihad — can lay claim to being truly Turkish (48).

One thus discovers in Gabriel's struggles a move toward a reconciliation with his "spiritual" people and against the "secular" Turks. For Werfel, people who give up the search for religious meaning would always feel, and be, alienated. Because spirituality was important to Werfel, the religious Gabriel represents the virtues of cultural synthesis, but the secular Young Turks embody the horrors of it. Like other *völkisch* thinkers, asserts Steiman, Werfel understood religiosity as a moral force that constantly renews the spiritual ties to one's heritage and thus centers the individual in an otherwise confusing world (93). Werfel considered Gabriel heroic because he comes to recognize the importance of belonging to a particular culture with a particular tradition and religion. Gabriel puts his Western training to use in self-sacrificing service to his people, because he rediscovers their importance to him in a grander, spiritual scheme of things:

> Vater und Sohn im Morgenland! Das läßt sich kaum mit der oberflächlichen Beziehung zu Eltern und Kindern in Europa vergleichen. Wer seinen Vater sieht, sieht Gott. Denn dieser Vater ist das letzte Glied der ununterbrochenen Ahnenkette, die den Menschen mit Adam und dadurch mit dem Ursprung der Schöpfung verbindet. Doch auch, wer seinen Sohn sieht, sieht Gott. Denn dieser Sohn ist das nächste Glied, welches den Menschen mit dem jüngsten Gericht, dem Ende aller Dinge und der Erlösung verbindet. (25–6)

> (Father and son in the East! It can scarcely be compared with the superficial relationship between European parents and children. Whoever sees his father sees God. For that father is the last link in a long, unbroken, ancestral chain, which connects all men to Adam, and therefore to the beginning of creation. At the same time, whoever sees his son sees God. For this son is the next link, which binds humans to the Final Judgment, the end of all things, redemption.)

Gabriel thereby saves their lives and his; he is renewed and strengthened in the knowledge that his destiny is shared with all of Armenian history. He successfully and positively assimilates what he has learned from the West into his understanding of himself as an Armenian. In the process he overcomes much of his feeling of alienation and attains a sense of meaning in his life. Becoming receptive to God allows Gabriel to work for and with his community. The spiritual message on the Armenian coin the Agha gives Gabriel thus strengthens his resolve on the Musa Dagh: "Dem Unerklärlichen in uns und über uns" (To the incomprehensible in us and beyond us) (47, 335).

The reader is never introduced to a Muslim equivalent of Gabriel. None of the Turks in Werfel's novel are able to arrive at the same kind of positive integration of Western and Oriental values that Gabriel achieves. Werfel's heroic Turks are those who have been entirely unaffected by Western culture. As members of a powerful empire, they can either be admired in their "pristine" state, or deplored in their "corrupted" one: there is no alternative.[11] In creating such dichotomies, Werfel reproduced much of the imperialistic logic that Europe was espousing at a time when it was actively colonizing the Islamicate world. Although the Germans did not actually colonize it, their attitudes — like those of other Europeans — toward the Islamicate world often mirrored an imperialistic mentality. In fact, Werfel's attitudes toward the Jewish settlers in Palestine also mirrored the sometimes contradictory logic of the imperialistic European powers toward this region. While he expressed disdain for the technological achievements of the West — and the Jews he believed were at the forefront of them — Werfel paradoxically came to appreciate the Zionists for their development of Palestine: there European-trained people with a moral and communal mission had revitalized an Orient supposedly grown fallow and corrupt. Likewise, in *Musa Dagh*, Werfel condemns the Armenians for bringing Western ideas to the Orient while making it clear that their ability to do so proves that they are superior to the other Orientals.

Werfel's attitude about the Orient was ambivalent, not unlike that of many Orientalists.[12] He implied that, whereas Western culture could benefit those Orientals who could keep it in proper perspective and remain deeply religious, not all Orientals should be privy to Western ideas, because they might become too unpredictable and thus dangerous. Because he had internalized many of the negative stereotypes about Orientals, Werfel seems to have felt the same ambivalence toward his own Jewish heritage. Werfel's celebration of culture as a religious experience ended up reproducing — rather than challenging — the conservative *völkisch* German values of the dominant culture in which he was living as a member of an increasingly oppressed minority in 1933. His inability to evaluate Oriental culture by any means other than those constructed by a hostile German society left him in a quandary: while using the language and the logic of those Germans who silence and oppress people by defining them as inferior or Other, Werfel inadvertently reiforced his own marginalization as a Jewish-German.

Site where Werfel's nanny often took young Franz: crucifix erected by a repentant Jew who had mocked Christianity, Charles Bridge, Prague.
Photo by V. Schubel, 1991.

6: Conclusion

DESPITE THEIR SIMILARITIES as German Jewish authors rooted in expressionism, Else Lasker-Schüler, Friedrich Wolf, and Franz Werfel constructed very different images of the Orient in their works. Their constructions emerged out of the larger context of German Orientalist literary trends and out of the more specific debates among Jewish-Germans about their supposed relationship with Oriental culture. Their divergent visions of the East mirrored the different self-perceptions of Jewish-Germans in the years 1900 and 1933.

All three authors revealed to their German readers what they considered to be positive aspects of Oriental culture. They hoped to affirm certain values — values important to each of them in their individual situations as Jewish-Germans. For Lasker-Schüler, the Orient was filled with liminal, visionary artists like herself; it served as the vehicle by which she explored her role as a Jewish artist in a German society. For Wolf, the Orient was the birthplace of a great message of social justice espoused by Islam; here he came to understand his political position as a Jew in a war-torn German society. For Werfel the Orient abounded with opportunities for exploring one's religiosity; it is where he came to terms with his identity as a controversial Jewish-Christian thinker in a German society. For all three authors the Orient was an imaginative sphere where they could describe and come to terms with their positions in German society. In this regard they were not so different from other, non-Jewish, German artists who thought they were coming to terms with different cultural values by experimenting with exoticism but were actually coming to terms with themselves. And yet, their Jewishness made this process especially complicated, and their supposedly Oriental identities meant that they necessarily had more at stake than their non-Jewish counterparts in writing Orientalist literature.

Else Lasker-Schüler's Orientalist literary works reflect a fascination for the exotic, the mythical, and the mystical. The stories in *Die Nächte Tino von Bagdads* and *Der Prinz von Theben* mix elements from Judaic and Muslim traditions in an amorphous Orient. Lasker-Schüler saw herself in a unique position, as a Jewish-German woman, to transmit a heterogeneous Oriental culture to the German reader. In her collections of Orientalist stories she expressed a wish to serve as a bridge for a spiritual union between West and East. At this time Lasker-Schüler regularly dressed in androgynous, Turkish costumes and told people that she came from the areas she wrote about; she even adopted the personas of both Tino, Princess of Baghdad, and Jussuf, Prince of Thebes. As a female, Jewish, impoverished, bohemian artist, Lasker-Schüler understood her marginality in German culture. She sought and found in the Orient an imaginative space where she could explore and celebrate her difference — a space where her Otherness would make sense. By employing Oriental settings, Lasker-Schüler was able to use exoticism to create a sphere for developing her nontraditional ideas about aesthetics and to redefine her role in German society as "special" in a positive sense.

Lasker-Schüler reproduced many of those stereotypes that made it difficult for Germans to identify, or at least sympathize, with Oriental culture. She strengthened, rather than subverted, the boundary between East and West. Even when she avoided clichés, she produced images that were too esoteric for her readers. Her imaginings appeared self-indulgent and brooding: no one else could fathom how she suffered as a result of her cultural and artistic uniqueness. Rather than underscoring the recognition that all peoples — regardless of their cultural identities — can develop an appreciation for one another, Lasker-Schüler makes it difficult for German readers to view Orientals (and thus herself) as anything other than alien.

Friedrich Wolf's Orientalism in *Mohammed: Ein Oratorium* is perhaps the most complex of the authors examined here. Like other Orientalist German authors, Wolf ended up using Oriental culture to suit his own needs. On the one hand, his retelling of Muhammad's biography can be seen as pure appropriation because he added and omitted elements from the Prophet's life to suit his artistic needs. The European Wolf used the exotic nature of the story to explore his own identity issues and felt he had the right to depict Islamic history as he saw fit — an attitude Muslims might find typical of offensive European Orientalism. Further, because he used Muhammad as an example, he left out those parts of the Prophet's biography that complicated Wolf's concerns. For example, even if he was depicted as nonviolent until his departure for Medina, Muhammad later came to accept the necessity of using armed struggle to defend the faith. By ending the play before this event, Wolf could paint Muhammad as the epitome of a nonviolent revolutionary; he was also able to avoid having to examine the conflicts that later arose between Muhammad and the Jews of Medina. Instead, Wolf's *Mohammed* was able to emphasize the unity of Jews and Muslims.

Wolf's Orientalism is enigmatic because he was not interested in dwelling on Muhammad's Otherness. It is not Muhammad's exoticism that Wolf found attractive: Wolf praised *universal* aspects of Muhammad's character and message. To Wolf, Muhammad was a hero because Muhammad recognized the world needed changing, he set out to do it, and he succeeded. Wolf, too, wanted to change the world — or at least what he considered to be the intolerant, greedy, violent society of which he was a member. In order to do so, Wolf recognized that he had to study similar circumstances in human history. Without an appreciation of the common bonds shared by all of humanity, Wolf realized, personal and social transformation is not possible. Muhammad's example shows that self-realization is not sufficient: although it is essential for people to grapple with their religious and cultural beliefs, the lessons learned from this process must be applied to improving the world around them. This is what Wolf gleaned from the Prophet, and it is what he wished to convey in the drama about him. Wolf's respect for Muhammad, and his willingness to celebrate cultural difference without losing sight of the universal ties that bind peoples of all traditions, make *Mohammed* unique in German Orientalist fiction of this period.

The Orient was both repulsive and attractive to Franz Werfel. With his characterizations in *Die vierzig Tage des Musa Dagh*, Werfel constructed a hierarchy of Otherness based upon categorizing certain human qualities as inherently Eastern or Western. Complicating a clear preference of West over East, Werfel erected a hierarchy of positive and negative paradigms about the Orient that he ultimately modified through his religious perspective. He criticized the Young Turks because they became secular and Westernized, while he commended traditional Armenians and Sufis because they remained devoutly religious and premodern. The hero of the novel, however, is a Westernized Oriental who rediscovers the importance of his people's history and religion. Gabriel's renewed faith and his understanding of the importance of tradition, combined with his Western training and expertise, make him a savior of his people. Under his guidance, his village (and, therefore, culture) escapes annihilation.

Werfel's depiction of Oriental culture and history was fraught with traditional German stereotypes. His celebration of culture as a religious experience reproduced many of the values of the conservative German culture in which he lived as a member of an oppressed minority. Werfel was attempting to depict what he saw as paradigmatically West and East in *Musa Dagh*. Yet these conventions did not further his aim of promoting cultural understanding. In his efforts to produce "typical" Asians and Europeans (albeit with differentiations between those who are religious and those who are secular), Werfel resorted to commonplace views that work against the empathy for the Armenians he wished to elicit in his German readership. Werfel ended up erecting both ethno-Orientalist and ethno-Occidentalist constructions because he identified at various points with both the Armenians and the Europeans in his novel; James Carrier defines "ethno-Orientalism" as formulaic depictions of Eastern cultures used by members of those societies themselves, and "ethno-Occidentalism" as stereotypical characterizations of the West by Orientals (198). Like many of the portrayals of Orientals in the history of

German Orientalist fiction, Werfel's characterizations demonstrate their shallowness. For, like Lasker-Schüler, rather than carefully delineate the complexities that shape people, Werfel reinforced traditional German conventions about the differences between East and West.

According to most scholars and biographers, Else Lasker-Schüler was primarily a Jewish poet; that is, hers was fundamentally the voice of marginalized, Jewish outsiders living in German society. Abdul JanMohamed's understanding of Said's concepts of "home" and "home-lessness" help to explain Lasker-Schüler's insistence on being seen literally and metaphorically as homeless in Germany. He asserts that having a home implies that a person belongs to one particular culture; homelessness suggests that one has fallen through the cracks of culture, is marginalized by it — at best, one lives on the borders of it. As isolating an experience as being homeless is, however, it can be extremely liberating. JanMohamed explains that, because being homeless means occupying a cultural space that has not yet been fully claimed or determined in any way by a majority society, it presents "a situation wherein utopian potentiality can endure" ("Worldliness" 110). One might therefore expect that, as a homeless border intellectual, Lasker-Schüler would be able to transcend typical German cultural paradigms when writing about other Others, especially other Orientals. However, Lasker-Schüler's neoromantic notion of being able to synthe-size the best of the Orient and the best of the Occident emerges as highly problematic. Despite the fact that she saw herself as a bridge between East and West, she merely used German commonplace notions about the Orient, and even reinforced these stereotypes about the supposed differences between cultures. Lasker-Schüler thus showed her-self to be a European author rather than an Asian one.

Similarly, the case of Franz Werfel proves troublesome. One might suppose that, as an assimilated German, he would unthinkingly reproduce German cliches about the Orient without any regard for the perspective of those marginalized by that society. Yet he challenged the perspective that assimilated, Westernized Others should be emulated. Werfel showed sympathy for the argument that oppressed people must integrate the values of their traditional culture with the values of their adopted culture. But Werfel resorted to stereotypical German — and even *völkisch* — notions to make this point. Partha Chatterjee explains the problematic nature of implicitly accepting a Western critique of Orientals, even if those assumptions are used in the service of an anti-colonialist agenda: in the long run, this strategy works against attempts to understand other cultures in newer, more insightful ways (194–5). Werfel's use of conventional notions about the "spiritual" East and the "rational" West further strengthens these false dichotomies, and this is precisely what is disturbing about his novel. The problem with his approach is that it does not challenge any of the basic assumptions

Germans have about Orientals — or even that of Werfel himself, as an Oriental Jewish-German — as being exotic. The culturally transcendent moment he hoped to achieve between peoples through a heightened sense of spirituality is simply not available to all: culture, like the world, is divided for Werfel into two parts. Werfel used his *völkisch* conservatism to simply underscore supposed differences between peoples, rather than bring them more closely together. According to Werfel's novel, except for the rare individual like Gabriel, most of us are destined to live our lives as spiritually barren but sociopolitically progressive followers of a Western path, or as spiritually rich but sociopolitically stagnant followers of an Eastern one. Opening and integrating these two paths seems impossible for most people — presumably even Jewish-Germans.

Finally, one might presume the least amount of empathy for another culture to come from Friedrich Wolf, who perhaps was regarded by his German contemporaries as one of the most assimilated Jewish-German writers of this era. Henning Müller points out that even today most Germans either do not know or do not think it important that Wolf was Jewish (*Arzt*, 5). He had been active in the *völkisch* Youth movements and had been proudly nationalistic about his German identity. However, of our three authors, Wolf proved best able to empathize with an Oriental Other and transcend German stereotypes in *Mohammed*. Despite what scholars may have thought, Wolf was conscious of being both a Jew and a political dissident in German society. He communicated a point of view that effectively expressed the experiences of being an outsider, and he revealed the potential benefits of seeing the world through the eyes of a border intellectual: Wolf feels at home in a variety of cultural contexts while maintaining the advantages of being homeless in them all.

The artist who can best oscillate continually is one who is at home — in other words, is somehow comfortable — in the interplay between cultures. JanMohamed clarifies that this kind of artist has the ability to recast the borders into a state of "*homelessness-as-home*" by turning a negative determination (the status of an outsider or marginalized border intellectual) into a positive vocation, mining that site for its political and epistomological wealth" ("Worldliness" 112–13). Among the other writers examined here, Wolf's attitude best reflected a "noncoercive" approach to knowledge, which, according to Said, is the "open and generous" approach to studying other cultures that distinguishes a great intellectual (112).

Like Lasker-Schüler and Werfel, Wolf indicated the various cultural borders to be crossed by Jewish-Germans in the early twentieth century. But unlike the works of Lasker-Schüler or Werfel, Wolf's drama reveals that he is more comfortable with — and even excited by — being a person with multiple identities. Wolf was able to see in Muhammad's struggles that most people throughout history have grappled with simultaneously occupying numerous positions in their societies.

Although Wolf was banned by the Nazis and "excommunicated" by most U.S. and West German scholars because of his communist politics, his best dramas — *Mohammed*, *Der arme Konrad*, *Cyankali*, and *Professor Mamlock* — are among the more interesting from the Weimar Republic. Now that the Cold War is over, Wolf should be reexamined in the light of the respect he earned in his day as a playwright and humanitarian. It is owing to Wolf's remarkable insights into the complexities of the politics of identity that academics should include Wolf in their course syllabi. He deserves to be valued once again for his many contributions instead of merely being relegated the dishonorable status of "Markus Wolf's father." For Wolf, it is the ability of people to cross real and imagined borders that linked his life and situation to Muhammad's and even, perhaps, to peoples of all times and cultures to each other. This ability — to see cultural differences while still recognizing universal human similarities — makes Wolf's drama emancipatory for both the author and his audience.

Notes

Orientalism and Jewish-German Identity

1. Edward Said refers to three different uses for the term Orientalism: the changing historical and cultural relationship between Europe and Asia, the scientific discipline in the West specializing in the study of various Oriental cultures, and European ideological suppositions, images, and fantasies about the Orient (Said, "Reconsidered" 90). This book will explore the third definition of Orientalism as it applies to German fictional depictions of the Islamicate Orient.

2. There is an important distinction between the terms "Muslim" or "Islamic" and the (unfortunately less well-known) term "Islamicate." Marshall Hodgson distinguishes between "Islamicate" and "Islamic" (or "Muslim") in the following way: Islamicate refers to "a *culture* . . . distinctive of Islamdom the *society*, and which has been naturally shared in by both Muslims and non-Muslims who participate at all fully in the society . . . ."; Islamic (or Muslim) refers to the *religiously-based* culture of those who practice Islam, not "the far more general phenomena . . . [of] Islamicate cultural traditions" (58).

3. Sander Gilman has written extensively that he thinks Jews were seen as "Blacks" by Germans. See, for example, his *Jewish Self-Hatred*. My proposition is, I believe, a more basic and defensible one: that Jews were regarded as "Orientals," and this was the main obstacle to their struggle for acceptance as Germans.

4. For examples of older scholarship on German literary Orientalism, see A. Leslie Willson's *A Mythical Image: The Ideal of India in German Romanticism* or Katharina Mommsen's *Goethe und 1001 Nacht* [sic].

5. The newer style of scholarship on German Orientalism begins with Henry Remak's article "Exoticism in Romanticism." Remak argues that, since constructs of the exotic have always been relative and flexible, scholars need to take this into account when they attempt to analyze them in literature. A collection of essays entitled *Die andere Welt: Studien zum Exotismus* explores the possible reasons why certain German authors found different parts of the world to be exotic, and why this exoticism was appealing to them in particular historical contexts. The important publications which accompanied the 1987 Stuttgart exhibit entitled "Exotische Welten, Europäische Phantasien" (both the book by the same title and *Exotische Figuren und Motive im europäischen Theater*) contain over thirty essays which examine sundry aspects of European constructions of the exotic. These publications are extremely useful as reference guides, providing me with easy access to the various theoretical positions espoused by the essayists represented therein. Andrea Fuchs-Sumiyoshi's *Orientalismus in der deutschen Literatur* attempts to prove that - since Germans did not colonize the Orient like France and Great Britain - German authors did not necessarily "colonize" the Orient in their literature, even though they may have appropriated it. Ingeborg Solbrig's article on "Orientalismus im Expressionismus" illuminates the connections between the concerns of the expressionist literary

movement and its interest in the Orient. Cornelia Kleinlogel's *Erotik-Exotik* uses a Saidian framework to examine the *Sittengeschichte* of Germany through an analysis of its literary representations of Turks. Christiane Günther's *Aufbruch nach Asien* examines the intersections and divergences between German imperialistic aims and literary constructs of the East. And Ludwig Ammann's *Östliche Spiegel* explores the cultural and artistic reasons why German Romanticism was drawn to experimenting with Oriental culture.

6. Steven Aschheim's *Brothers and Strangers* traces the Orientalist overtones of the conflicts between the *Westjuden* and the *Ostjuden*. Michael Berkowitz's *Zionist Culture and West European Jewry before the First World War* interprets the Orientalist aspects (among others) of Zionist visual arts.

7. James Clifford perhaps best sums up the connection between Foucault and Said:

> Said extends Foucault's analysis to include ways in which a cultural order is defined externally, with respect to exotic "others." In an imperialist context definitions, representations, and textualizations of subject peoples and places play the same constitutive role as "internal" representations . . . and have the same consequences — discipline and confinement, both physical and ideological. Therefore "the Orient," in Said's analysis, exists uniquely *for* the Occident. His task in *Orientalism* is to dismantle the discourse, to expose its oppressive system, to "clear the archive" of its received ideas and static images. (265)

8. Walter Sokel, whose *The Writer in Extremis* inimitably examines the German expressionist artistic movement (1910–25), sums up the chief characteristics and tensions of expressionism in the following way:

> Expressionism as abstract form, as part of the modernist movement, and Expressionism as formless shriek arise from the same factor — subjectivism. This subjectivism in turn results from a peculiar social-constellation endemic to Germany since the eighteenth century. Germany was the homeland both of "autonomous art," abstractness in the best sense, and of a tradition of rhetorical formlessness, abstractness in the worst sense. This double aspect of abstractness also underlies Expressionism, which is firmly rooted in certain German traditions even though it rebels against others. But abstractness also underlies the whole phenomenon of modernism. . . . German Expressionism sought to be two things in one: a revolution of poetic form and vision, and a reformation of human life. (4, 225)

9. For background on Lasker-Schüler's life, I relied on the following sources: Dieter Bänsch's *Else Lasker-Schüler: Zur Kritik eines etablierten Bildes*; Sigrid Bauschinger's *Else Lasker-Schüler: Ihr Werk und ihre Zeit*, and her article "'Ich bin Jude. Gott sei Dank.' Else Lasker-Schüler" in *Im Zeichen Hiobs: Jüdische Schriftsteller und deutsche Literatur im 20. Jahrhundert*; Jakob Hessing's *Else Lasker-Schüler: Biographie einer deutsch-jüdischen Dichterin*; Judith Kuckart's *Im Spiegel der Bäche finde ich mein Bild nicht mehr: Gratwanderung einer anderen Ästhetik der Dichterin Else Lasker-Schüler*; and Mary-Elizabeth O'Brien's "'Ich war verkleidet als Poet . . . Ich bin Poetin!!': The Masquerade of Gender in Else Lasker-Schüler's Prose."

10. Lasker-Schüler's practice was to rename all her friends in ways she thought suited them better by describing their true, inner essence. Hence, Karl Kraus became "Dalai Lama," Gottfried Benn became the "Barbarian," Martin Buber became "Herr von Zion," etc.

11. For information on Wolf's biography, I used the following materials: Lew Hohmann's *Friedrich Wolf. Bilder einer deutschen Biographie*; Werner Jehser's *Friedrich Wolf. Sein Leben und Werk*; Henning Müller's *Friedrich Wolf: Weltbürger aus Neuwied, "Der jüdische Arzt und Kommunist Dr. Friedrich Wolf": Dokumente des Terrors und der Verfolgung 1931–1944*, and *Wer war Wolf?*; Walter Pollatschek's *Friedrich Wolf. Leben und Schaffen*; and Hans Rodenberg's "Der Weg Friedrich Wolfs" in *Auf wieviel Pferden ich geritten . . . Der junge Friedrich Wolf: Eine Dokumentation*.

12. The biographical information on Werfel came from the following sources: Norbert Abels's *Franz Werfel mit Selbstzeugnissen und Bilddokumenten*; Lore Foltin's *Franz Werfel*; Peter Jungk's *Franz Werfel: A Life in Prague, Vienna, and Hollywood*; Oskar Metzler's "Franz Werfel" in *Österreichische Literatur des 20. Jahrhunderts*; and Lionel Steiman's *Franz Werfel — The Faith of an Exile: From Prague to Beverly Hills*.

13. From the *Völkischer Beobachter*, Berlin, 27 February, 1931 (Müller 10).

14. I use the terms "German culture" and "German identity" similarly for the same reason. However, and despite the fact that I use these blanket terms, I do not regard Germans, German cultures, or German societies to be actually homogenous.

15. Again, just as one cannot claim that German identity was, in fact, homogenous, there was no single understanding of what it meant to be a Jewish-German.

16. See, for example, "Appendix I. A Short Political History of the Weimar Republic," in Peter Gay's excellent *Weimar Culture: The Outsider as Insider* for a brief overview of this era.

17. See George L. Mosse's *Germans and Jews* for an authoritative examination of *völkisch*ness.

18. Ruth Gay clarifies that German *Liberal* Judaism is equivalent to what is called Reform Judaism in the U.S. German *Reform* Judaism was a tiny movement centered in Berlin which stressed the similarities between it and Christianity (155).

19. Later, explains Mosse, Nazi propagandists used the notion that the Jews living amongst the Gentiles were Orientals to argue that these "Asiatic" Jews were secretly working to undermine the German way of life (*Germans* 47).

20. See John Murray Cuddihy's *The Ordeal of Civility*.

21. According to Donald Niewyk, Zionists were split on the issue of whether their connection to the East should extend to seeing "racial" ties to the Arabs. For some this step theoretically made sense, but for others their cultural ties to Europe made this notion inconceivable (133–34).

Imagining the Orient

1. The proper English transliteration of the Prophet's name is Muhammad. I will accordingly use this spelling of his name except when referring to German titles of literature, including Wolf's play *Mohammed*.

2. See especially Wolfgang Köhler's study on the impact of *1001 Nights* on German Orientalist literature.

3. This coincides with the Western idea that Europe has a history, whereas the Orient does not.

4. Zulima in fact allows him to construct the Orient on his terms, which suit Novalis's Romantic program. Heinrich thus does not really learn anything from her at all; he, the Romantic poet-priest, is already both the conqueror and knower of the Orient.

5. For more on the Romantics' notion of the Orient, see Ammann's *Östliche Spiegel*.

6. In Germany, the "Egyptian" novels of Paul Scheerbart and Georg Ebers were particularly popular (Bauschinger, *Else* 101).

7. For a discussion of the influence of Orientalism on French experimental literature, see Beryl Schlossman's *The Orient of Style: Modernist Allegories of Conversion*.

8. Goethe's *West-östlicher Diwan* stands out as an example of this phenomenon in German literature.

9. For an extended discussion of this response, see Christiane Günther's *Aufbruch nach Asien*.

10. See Ella Shohat's "Antinomies of Exile."

Else Lasker-Schüler's Oriental Performance Space

1. Both of these texts underwent minor revision when they were reissued. *Die Nächte Tino von Bagdads* was reissued in 1919 as *Die Nächte der Tino von Bagdads*; *Der Prinz von Theben* was reissued in 1920 as *Der Prinz von Theben: Ein Geschichtenbuch*. Although I have all the versions of these texts at my disposal, I use the later versions because the earlier versions contain more mistakes (misspellings, etc.). Whereas some of the poems in the original version of *Die Nächte* were omitted in the second version, the differences in the stories themselves in both *Die Nächte* and *Der Prinz* are negligible.

2. For information on the biographical sources I used for understanding Lasker-Schüler's life, see note 9 in the introduction.

3. For the critical reception of Lasker-Schüler's artistic productions, I relied on the following sources: Dieter Bänsch's *Else Lasker-Schüler: Zur Kritik eines etablierten Bildes*; Sigrid Bauschinger's *Else Lasker-Schüler: Ihr Werk und ihre Zeit* and "'Ich bin Jude. Gott sei Dank,' Else Lasker-Schüler." in *Im Zeichen Hiobs: Jüdische Schriftsteller und deutsche Literatur im 20. Jahrhundert*; Jakob Hessing's *Else Lasker-Schüler: Biographie einer deutsch-jüdischen Dichterin*; Wieland Herzfelde's "Else Lasker-Schüler. Begegnungen mit der Dichterin" in *Sinn und Form*; Judith Kuckart's *Im Spiegel der Bäche finde ich mein Bild nicht mehr: Gratwanderung einer anderen Ästhetik der Dichterin Else Lasker-Schüler*; Mary-Elizabeth O'Brien's "'Ich war verkleidet als Poet . . . Ich bin Poetin!!': The Masquerade of Gender in Else Lasker-Schüler's Prose"; and Meir Wiener's "Else Lasker-Schüler" in *Juden in der deutschen Literatur: Essays über zeitgenössische Schriftsteller*.

4. Because several other critical studies exist about Lasker-Schüler's position as a woman, a Jew, or a bohemian in German society, I focus more on her relationship with Orientalism, which has remained relatively unexplored. Of course, all the above characteristics of Lasker-Schüler factor into her Orientalism.

5. Neither *Die Nächte* nor *Der Prinz* contain a coherent frame story, which makes them quite different from *1001 Nights*. For more on the influence of *1001 Nights* on German literature, see Wolfgang Köhler.

6. This aesthetic stance played into a phenomenon documented by Rana Kabbani (among others) as particular to experimental European artists:

> If the language of ordinary description has been overworked and overburdened, then the only outlet is figurative language, the substitution of metaphor and reverie. The Orient becomes a pretext for self-dramatization

and differentness; it is the malleable theatrical space in which can be played out . . . egocentric fantasies . . . . It affords endless material for the imagination and endless potential for the Occidental self. (11)

7. Of course, to a certain extent, Wiener's characterization of Lasker-Schüler's style is correct. In both *Die Nächte* and *Der Prinz*, she often makes excessively cryptic references, and her representations of Oriental culture often border on *kitsch*. But it does not follow that these works cannot be regarded as art: these traits are found in most of the German Orientalist art from this period, and Lasker-Schüler's is certainly some of the most poetic and moving literature of the genre. I am interested in what Lasker-Schüler believes she is expressing when she employs this "dilettante" style, and how this relates to the larger context of German Orientalism. The masks worn by Lasker-Schüler, whether they are a sign of her dilettantism as an artist or not, allowed her to shape for herself a positive identity as an Oriental, German-speaking Jew in an often hostile environment.

8. With her concept of the *Wildjude*, Lasker-Schüler also plays into parts of the European "noble savage" tradition.

9. Although it is normally considered taboo to assume the narrator and the author are the same person, I do so with Lasker-Schüler because she adopted the personas of her narrators in her own life. For example, during the time when she was writing the stories of Tino and narrating them through Tino's voice, she was also going by the name Tino and dressing like her in everyday life.

10. It is unclear who the narrator of the story "Der Tempel Jehovah" (The Temple of Jehovah) is. While it is probably Tino, the Jewish theme would be inconsistent with her religious identity as a Muslim.

11. The standard transliteration of Joseph from Hebrew is Yossef. Giving him an Arabic name and Jewish identity establishes him as a bridge between the two cultures and underscores the unifying role Joseph plays between the Egyptians and the Israelites in the Hebrew Bible.

12. For a discussion of the possible gender implications of this switch, see Mary-Elizabeth O'Brien's essay, note 3, above.

13. Of course, Lasker-Schüler plays here with the image of a crescent moon with a star, the well-known emblem of Islamicate cultures.

14. Tragically, this feeling was concretely realized during the Nazi period, when Lasker-Schüler was forced into exile, first in Switzerland and then in Palestine.

15. The significance of this is illuminated by bell hooks: "Cross-dressing, appearing in drag, transsexualism, are all choices that emerge in a context where the notion of subjectivity is challenged . . . where identity is always perceived as capable of construction, invention, change" (Juno 80). In this context, it is the readers' notions of subjectivity which are challenged.

16. However, Lasker-Schüler's descriptions of "actual" Sufis in the stories "Der Fakir von Theben" (The Fakir of Thebes), "Der Derwisch" (The Dervish), and "Der Fakir" (The Fakir) paint them as cruel, hypocritical, and dangerous. In so doing, she illustrates the problem presented by any mystical system: whereas Tino and Jussuf represent what a Sufi should be (Lasker-Schüler's mystical ideal), the access to power afforded by their position in the religious community corrupts the religious practices of the "real" Sufis in these texts.

17. See, for example, the poetry of Mevlana Rumi. His poetry, along with that of other great Persian Sufis, was widely read in the eighteenth century. Since Goethe, Lasker-

Schüler's literary hero, was an avid reader of such poetry, it is not inconceivable that she may have read some herself. Certainly she was at least familiar with these Sufis and their poetry from Goethe's writings.

18. Such notions are more often based on the projection of European fantasies than on any grain of historical "truth." For example, in "Ached Bey," dervishes dance in a mosque (DN 63), even though dervishes do not dance in mosques but in special buildings called tekkiyas. During the Shi'a commemoration of Muharram in "Der Dervish," she shows the entire city of Cairo engaged in a "Menschvergießen" (human blood-letting) (DP 102); actually, the Shi'a population in modern Egypt is very small, and Lasker-Schüler grossly exaggerates the intensity of the self-flagellation used by the Shi'a during their ritual practices. And blacks are only depicted throughout *Die Nächte* and *Der Prinz* as slaves occupying very subordinate positions, despite the fact that slavery based on race was a rare occurrence in the Islamicate world.

19. Quoted in Grunfeld (144).

An Oriental Role Model for Friedrich Wolf

1. *Mohammed* has never been performed. Wolf writes to his wife Else, in a letter dated April 4, 1925, that he has received a request from Bruno Schönfeld to stage *Mohammed* at the Anhalter Landestheater. Why this never happened remains unknown.

2. I am aware of three versions of Wolf's Muhammad drama. A scene from the first, which was originally entitled *Der Löwe Gottes* (The Lion of God), appeared in the periodical *Der wesentliche Leser* (The Essential Reader) in 1919. Wolf made minor changes in this, and the second version, entitled *Mohammed: Ein Oratorium*, was published by the Chronosverlag in 1924; to the best of my knowledge only three copies of this version still exist (my copy, a copy in the Friedrich-Wolf-Archiv, and a copy in the Deutscher Bücherei in Leipzig). The final version of Wolf's drama, entitled *Mohammed: Ein Schauspiel (Muhammad: A Play)*, was modified for the Aufbau Verlag in 1951. In this study, I am only interested in *Mohammed: Ein Oratorium* because it is the most complete version which reflects Wolf's earlier concerns and perspectives. Because very few people will have access to this version of Wolf's play, I have quoted liberally from it.

3. For an explanation of my spelling of the Prophet's name, see note one in "Imagining the Orient."

4. Wolf writes in his diary on a couple of occasions about his desire to travel to Asia. For example, in the fall of 1925, he planned a trip to what he called the awakening Orient. The trip was to have included stops in Alexandria, Jerusalem, Konya, Ankara, Azerbaijan, and Moscow. Although he finally made it to Moscow, where he lived in exile during the Nazi period, Wolf was never able to visit these other places.

5. For a discussion of this, see "Imagining the Orient," pp. 48–52.

6. See especially his long letter to Gustav Gerstenberger of October 12, 1916, where he expresses anger about the senselessness of the war (Wolf, *Auf wieviel Pferden* 121–27).

7. Quote from Friedrich Wolf in "Die Fahne Tragen" (1929) (reprinted in Hohmann 67). Note the wonderful religious, albeit Christian, imagery: this was the moment when Paul converted from Judaism to Christianity.

8. For the biographical sources I used about Wolf's life, see note 11 in the introduction.

9. Indeed, his grandmother boxed his ears once when Wolf and his young friends made fun of a group of refugees from Bessarabia — *Ostjuden*. Wolf claimed that this experience left a lasting impression on him. This incident also discloses the fact that Wolf experienced firsthand the tensions between the *Westjuden* and *Ostjuden* described by Steven Aschheim.

10. Meyer's twelfth letter, entitled "Vom Leben und Töten" (On Living and Killing) provides an interesting discussion about how it is sometimes justified to break the commandment "Thou shalt not kill" — for example, in the event of war. Meyer contradicts himself in this section, sometimes glorifying war, and sometimes bemoaning it. What he definitely condemns, however, are those who initiate war for greedy and base reasons. Because this last sentiment reverberates throughout *Mohammed*, it strikes me that Wolf might have referred to this letter while writing his play.

11. After divorcing his Jewish wife (Käthe Gumpold), Wolf married a Christian (Else Dreibholz) in 1923, which caused another family crisis — this time with his mother.

12. Letter to Käthe Gumpold, December 18, 1915 (Wolf, *Auf wieviel Pferden* 108).

13. In a letter to Herrmann Lewy (January 3, 1949), Wolf writes that he acknowledged his ancestors in two of his literary works: *Das Heldenlied des alten Bundes* (The Epic of the Old Covenant, 1925) and *Mohammed*.

14. Because of the rather tendentious style of *Mohammed*, most of the secondary literature dismisses it as nothing more than a typical, expressionist *Ideendrama* (drama about ideas). Wolf's two major biographers, Werner Jehser and Walther Pollatschek, have been especially influential in disseminating this point of view. As East German literary critics, they had much at stake in giving short shrift to Wolf's earlier (expressionist) works in order to concentrate on his later (socialist realist) ones.

West German critics have often disagreed with their East German counterparts on this matter. Ingeborg Solbrig, who also refers to *Mohammed* as a "typically expressionistic 'scream play,'" prefers the earlier version, claiming that Wolf's later version of the play "lacks the energy and immediacy of the original version" because it harps on social issues while adhering to the principles of socialist realism (2018). Hans Rodenberg, the editor of the latest collection of Wolf's letters, also takes issue with attacks on the early *Mohammed*. He refers to it as probably Wolf's most poetically rich play — these are people, not just facades for the author's political agenda — and claims if Wolf had continued to write this way, he could have reached his goals more thoroughly and quickly (459).

15. Wolf's two primary sources on Islam and Mohammed are Friedrich Delitzsch's *Die Welt des Islam* (The World of Islam, 1915) and Max Henning's introduction to his translation/interpretation of the Qur'an (*Der Koran*, 1901).

16. Letter from July 31, 1915 (Wolf, *Auf wieviel Pferden* 95).

17. See A. Guillaume's *The Life of Muhammed: A Translation of Ibn Tshaq's Sirat Rasul Allah* for traditional sources of the Prophet's biography.

18. In two letters to Wolf, Said Imam, who read the play when he was in Berlin, sang the praises of *Mohammed*. On April 2, 1930, he wrote from Damascus: "You have made me very happy with your *Mohammed*. I will think of you not only when I see or read your *Mohammed*, but also when I think about my Mohammed . . . ". On April 19 he wrote again, proclaiming, "My many Muslim friends are still disagreeing with each other about your *Mohammed*; . . . many think that it's really a shame that this play couldn't be performed!"

19. Diary entry of July 28, 1918.

20. Wolf's earlier enthusiasm for the existential aspects of Friedrich Nietzsche's philosophy resonates throughout this drama and confirms his connection to the expressionist literary movement.

21. Letter to Gustav Gerstenberger of August 1, 1918 (Wolf, *Auf wieviel Pferden* 180).

22. Letter to Gerstenberger of April 16, 1918 (Wolf, *Auf wieviel Pferden* 171).

23. This information comes from an interview I conducted with Michael Berkowitz at The Ohio State University on June 5, 1992. Berkowitz maintains that, because these periodicals (and others like them) were readily available in the Jewish students' reading rooms at the universities in Germany — and most Jewish students frequented these rooms — it was unavoidable for them to come into contact with images of Jews as Orientals.

24. Letter to Ida Wolf of July 31, 1915 (Wolf, *Auf wieviel Pferden* 97).

25. It is unclear in the play whether Gabriel transmits this to him or whether the words have been written directly by God into the clouds.

26. Letter to Gerstenberger of May 4, 1918 (Wolf, *Auf wieviel Pferden* 173–74).

"Bad" Orientals, "Good" Orientals, and Franz Werfel

1. Sokel argues that the novel *Verdi: Roman der Oper* (1923) signals Werfel's break with expressionism (222).

2. The sources on which I relied for Werfel's biographical details are listed in note 12 in the introduction.

3. On June 27, 1929, Werfel officially stopped practicing Judaism; on July 8, he married Alma Mahler.

4. Karl May's novels influenced Werfel to the extent that, when he was in Egypt, he referred back to May's depictions of the Orient when learning about the culture; he seemed disappointed that reality often did not live up to his expectations, based as they were on May's (and his) fantasies (Werfel, "ÄT" 711). Werfel himself wrote other Orientalist works of fiction besides *Musa Dagh*: "Esther, Kaiserin von Persien" (Esther, Empress of Persia, 1915) and "Der Dschin" (The Jinn, 1919) are representative.

5. *Musa Dagh* remains controversial to this day. According to Jungk, even though Werfel sold Hollywood (MGM) the film rights to it back in the 1940s, his novel has never been filmed; it appears that the Turkish government, the United States government, and others have put sufficient pressure on Hollywood to prevent Werfel's *Musa Dagh* from being filmed in the foreseeable future (147).

6. This also applies to the Arabs, who are occasionally mentioned. A group of people of mixed descent (Arab and Turkish) are even described as "die niedrigsten Parias des Propheten" (the lowest pariahs of the Prophet) (298).

7. These paradigms are discussed at length and throughout Edward Said's *Orientalism*.

8. For example, see Werfel's statements as quoted in Steiman (74–6).

9. Gunther Grimm remarks that in the novel one finds clear parallels between the oppressed Armenian minority and the persecuted Jewish people — not only do they share the same fate, but also the artistic and structural elements point to a symbolic integration of Jewish history (262).

10. See Lionel Steiman for an exegesis of Werfel's theological views on the role of the Jews in Christianity (168).

11. Maria Berl Lee, in her article "Agony, Pathos, and the Turkish Side," argues that Werfel's personal biases led him to write an account of this period that was historically inaccurate. In his zeal to side with a group with whom he could identify — people who were both victims of persecution and Christians — Werfel ignored all Turkish accounts of the Armenian genocide. Lee argues that the Armenians certainly were not deserving of their fate, but they were not innocent scapegoats taken by surprise as Werfel claimed. Lee's intention is to highlight a paradox in Werfel's logic: whereas he condemned the imperialism of the Young Turks, and even the Western ideas they imported and cultivated, he offered no criticism of those European imperialists with whom the Armenians sided; perhaps it is not generic imperialism Werfel wished to critique, but only a hybrid, Oriental/Western variety of it. However, Lee's argument is offensive: it is clear that a genocide did occur and — no matter what the Turkish government's intentions or reasons might have been — genocides can never be justified.

12. Edward Said discusses this ambivalence throughout *Orientalism*.

Works Consulted

Primary Sources

Delitzsch, Friedrich. *Die Welt des Islam*. Berlin: Ullstein, 1915.

Henning, Max. "Einleitung." *Der Koran*. Trans. Max Henning. Leipzig: Philipp Reclam, 1901.

Krojanker, Gustav, ed. *Juden in der deutschen Literatur: Essays über zeitgenössische Schriftsteller*. Berlin: Welt-Verlag, 1922.

———. "Vorwort des Herausgebers." *Juden in der deutschen Literatur: Essays über zeitgenössische Schriftsteller*. Ed. Gustav Krojanker. Berlin: Welt-Verlag, 1922.

Lasker-Schüler, Else. *Die Nächte der Tino von Bagdad*. In *Der Prinz von Theben und andere Prosa*. Munich: DTV, 1986.

———. *Der Prinz von Theben: Ein Geschichtenbuch*. In *Der Prinz von Theben und andere Prosa*. Munich: DTV, 1986.

Meyer, Moritz. *Sinai Briefe: Eine moderne Glosse von einem Rechtsgelehrten*. Neuwied: J. Meinckes, 1910.

Poeschel, Erwin. "Jakob Wassermann." *Juden in der deutschen Literatur: Essays über zeitgenössische Schriftsteller*. Ed. Gustav Krojanker. Berlin: Welt-Verlag, 1922.

Schach, Fabius. "Ost und West." *Ost und West* 3,9 (1903): 573–88.

Wassermann, Jakob. "Der Jude als Orientale." *Daimon* 1,1 (1918): 28–32.

Wolf, Friedrich. *Auf wieviel Pferden ich geritten . . . Der junge Friedrich Wolf: Eine Dokumentation*. Ed. Emmi Wolf and Brigitte Struzyk. Berlin: Aufbau, 1988.

———. "Der Loewe Gottes." *Der wesentliche Leser* 2,7 (December 1919): 1.

———. *Mohammed: Ein Oratorium*. Ludwigsburg: Chronosverlag, 1924.

———. *Mohammed: Ein Schauspiel*. In *Dramen*. Vol. 1. Ed. Else Wolf and Walther Pollatschek. Berlin: Aufbau, 1960.

Wolfenstein, Alfred. "Das neue Dichtertum des Juden." *Juden in der deutschen Literatur: Essays über zeitgenössische Schriftsteller*. Ed. Gustav Krojanker. Berlin: Welt-Verlag, 1922.

Werfel, Franz. "Ägyptisches Tagebuch." *Zwischen Oben und Unten*. Ed. Adolf Klarmann. Munich: Langen Müller, 1975.

———. *Die vierzig Tage des Musa Dagh*. Frankfurt: Fischer Taschenbuch, 1990.

Secondary Sources

Methodology and Background

Ammann, Ludwig. Östliche Spiegel: Ansichten vom Orient im Zeitalter seiner Entdeckung durch den deutschen Leser 1800–1850. Hildesheim: Georg Olms, 1989.

Aschheim, Steven E. Brothers and Strangers: The East European Jew in German and German Jewish Consciousness 1800–1923. Madison: U Wisconsin P, 1982.

Berkowitz, Michael. Zionist Culture and Western European Jewry before the First World War. Cambridge, UK: Cambridge UP, 1993.

Carrier, James G. "Occidentalism: the world turned upside- down." american ethnologist 19, 2 (May 1992): 195–212.

Chatterjee, Partha. "Their Own Words? An Essay for Edward Said." Edward Said: A Critical Reader. Ed. Michael Sprinkler. Cambridge, MA: Blackwell, 1992.

Clifford, James. The Predicament of Culture. Cambridge: Harvard UP, 1988.

Cuddihy, John Murray. The Ordeal of Civility: Freud, Marx, Levi-Strauss, and the Jewish Struggle with Modernity. New York: Basic Books, 1974.

Fuchs-Sumiyoshi, Andrea. Orientalismus in der deutschen Literatur: Untersuchungen zu Werken des 19. und 20. Jahrhunderts, von Goethe's West-östlichem Divan bis Thomas Manns Joseph-Tetralogie. Hildesheim: Georg Olms, 1984.

Gay, Peter. "Appendix I. A Short Political History of the Weimar Republic." Weimar Culture: The Outsider as Insider. New York: Harper Torchbooks, 1968.

——. "Introduction." In Ruth Gay. The Jews of Germany: A Historical Portrait. New Haven: Yale UP, 1992.

Gay, Ruth. The Jews of Germany: A Historical Portrait. New Haven: Yale UP, 1992.

Gilman, Sander L. Inscribing the Other. Lincoln, NE: U Nebraska P, 1991.

——. Jewish Self-Hatred. Baltimore: Johns Hopkins UP, 1986.

Grunfeld, Frederic V. Prophets without Honour: A Background to Freud, Kafka, Einstein and Their World. New York: Holt, Rinehart, and Winston, 1979.

Günther, Christiane C. Aufbruch nach Asien: Kulturelle Fremde in der deutschen Literatur um 1900. Munich: iudicium, 1988.

Hodgson, Marshall G.S. The Venture of Islam: Conscience and History in a World Civilization. Volume I: The Classical Age of Islam. Chicago: U Chicago P, 1974.

JanMohamed, Abdul. "The Economy of Manichean Allegory: The Function of Racial Difference in Colonialist Literature." "Race," Writing, and Difference. Ed. Henry Louis Gates, Jr. Chicago: U of Chicago P, 1985.

——. "Worldliness-Without-World, Homelessness-As-Home: Toward a Definition of the Specular Border Intellectual." Edward Said: A Critical Reader. Ed. Michael Sprinkler. Cambridge, MA: Blackwell, 1992.

Juno, Andrea. "bell hooks." Angry Women. Ed. Andrea Juno and V. Vale. San Francisco: Re/Search, 1991.

Kabbani, Rana. Europe's Myths of Orient. Bloomington: Indiana UP, 1986.

Kaplan, Marion A. The Making of the Jewish Middle Class: Women, Family, and Identity in Imperial Germany. New York: Oxford UP, 1991.

Kleinlogel, Cornelia. Exotik-Erotik: Zur Geschichte des Türkenbildes in der deutschen Literatur der frühen Neuzeit (1453–1800). Frankfurt/Main: Peter Lang, 1989.

Koebner, Thomas and Gerhart Pickerodt, eds. Die andere Welt: Studien zum Exotismus. Frankfurt/Main: Athenäum, 1987.

Köhler, Wolfgang. Hugo von Hofmannsthal und "TausendeineNacht": Untersuchungen zur Rezeption des Orients im epischen und essayistischen Werk. Mit einem einleitenden Überblick über den Einfluß von "Tausendeine Nacht" auf die deutsche Literatur. Frankfurt/Main: Peter Lang, 1972.

Kreidt, Dietrich. Exotische Figuren und Motive im europäischen Theater. Stuttgart: Institut für Auslandsbeziehungen, 1987.

Mattenklott, Gert. "Ostjudentum und Exotismus." Die andere Welt: Studien zum Exotismus. Ed. Thomas Koebner and Gerhart Pickerodt. Frankfurt/Main: Athenäum, 1987.

Mommsen, Katharina. Goethe und 1001 Nacht. Frankfurt/Main: Suhrkamp, 1981.

Mosse, George L. Germans and Jews. New York: Howard Fertig, 1970.

——. German Jews beyond Judaism. Cincinnati: Hebrew Union College P, 1985.

Niewyk, Donald L. The Jews in Weimar Germany. Baton Rouge: Louisiana State UP, 1980.

Osterwold, Tilman. "Faszination und Zerstörung — Anpassung und Unterwerfung." Exotische Welten, Europäische Phantasien. Ed. Tilman Osterwold and Hermann Pollig. Stuttgart: Institut für Auslandsbeziehungen Württembergischer Kunstverein, 1987.

Osterwold, Tilman and Hermann Pollig, eds. Exotische Welten, Europäische Phantasien. Stuttgart: Institut für Auslandsbeziehungen Württembergischer Kunstverein, 1987.

Pollig, Hermann. "Exotische Welten, Europäische Phantasien." Exotische Welten, Europäische Phantasien. Ed. Tilman Osterwold and Hermann Pollig. Stuttgart: Institut für Auslandsbeziehungen Württembergischer Kunstverein, 1987.

Raabe, Paul, Ed. Der Kampf um eine literarische Bewegung. Munich: DTV, 1965.

Remak, Henry H. H. "Exoticism in Romanticism." Comparative Literature Studies 15, 1 (1978): 53–65.

Said, Edward. Orientalism. New York: Vintage, 1978.

———. "Orientalism Reconsidered." Cultural Critique 1 (Fall 1985): 89–107.

Schick, Irvin Cemil. "Representing Middle Eastern Women: Feminism and Colonial Discourse." Feminist Studies 16, 2 (Summer 1990): 345–80.

Schlossman, Beryl. The Orient of Style: Modernist Allegories of Conversion. Durham, NC: Duke UP, 1991.

Schubel, Vernon James. Religious Practice in Contemporary Islam: Shi'i Devotional Rituals in South Asia. Columbia, SC: U South Carolina P, 1993.

Shohat, Ella. "Antinomies of Exile: Said at the Frontiers of National Narrations." Edward Said: A Critical Reader. Ed. Michael Sprinkler. Cambridge, MA: Blackwell, 1992.

Sokel, Walter. The Writer in Extremis: Expressionism in Twentieth-Century German Literature. Stanford: Stanford UP, 1959.

Solbrig, Ingeborg. "'Da las er: so, daß sich der Engel bog.' Zu Rilkes Gedicht 'Mohammeds Berufung' (1907)." Modern Austrian Literature 13, 3 (1980): 33–45.

———. "Literarischer Orientalismus im Expressionismus: Der Mohammed-Roman Klabunds." Im Dialog mit der Moderne. Ed. Roland Jost and Hansgeorg Schmidt-Bergmann. Frankfurt/Main: Athenäum, 1986.

———. "Die Rezeption des Gedichts 'Mahomets-Gesang' bei Goethes Zeitgenossen und in der modernen persischen Adaption Muhammed Iqbals (1923)." Goethe Jahrbuch 100 (1983): 111–26.

Turner, Victor and Edith. "Religious Celebrations." Celebration. Ed. Victor Turner. Washington, DC: Smithsonian, 1982.

Wicke, Jennifer and Michael Sprinkler. "Interview With Edward Said." Edward Said: A Critical Reader. Ed. Michael Sprinkler. Cambridge, MA: Blackwell, 1992.

Willson, A. Leslie. A Mythical Image: The Ideal of India in German Romanticism. Durham, NC: Duke UP, 1964.

Else Lasker-Schüler

Bänsch, Dieter. Else Lasker-Schüler: Zur Kritik eines etablierten Bildes. Stuttgart: J.B. Metzler, 1971.

Bauschinger, Sigrid. Else Lasker-Schüler: Ihr Werk und ihre Zeit. Heidelberg: Lothar Stiehm, 1980.

——. "'Ich bin Jude. Gott sei Dank,' Else Lasker-Schüler." Im Zeichen Hiobs: Jüdische Schriftsteller und deutsche Literatur im 20. Jahrhundert. Ed. Gunter Grimm, Hans-Peter Bayerdorfer, and Konrad Kwiet. Königstein/Ts.: Athenäum, 1985.

Hessing, Jakob. Else Lasker-Schüler: Biographie einer deutsch-jüdischen Dichterin. Karlsruhe: von Loeper, 1985.

Herzfelde, Wieland. "Else Lasker-Schüler. Begegnungen mit der Dichterin." Sinn und Form 21,6 (1969): 1294–1325.

Kuckart, Judith. Im Spiegel der Bäche finde ich mein Bild nicht mehr: Gratwanderung einer anderen Ästhetik der Dichterin Else Lasker-Schüler. Frankfurt/Main: S. Fischer, 1985.

O'Brien, Mary-Elizabeth. "'Ich war verkleidet als Poet . . . Ich bin Poetin!!': The Masquerade of Gender in Else Lasker-Schüler's Prose." Manuscript for Division on "Women Writing Men: Female Authors and Male Protagonists." MLA Convention. Chicago, 30 Dec. 1990.

Wiener, Meir. "Else Lasker-Schüler." Juden in der deutschen Literatur: Essays über zeitgenössische Schriftsteller. Ed. Gustav Krojanker. Berlin: Welt-Verlag, 1922.

Friedrich Wolf

Guillaume, A. The Life of Muhammed: A Translation of Ibn Tshaq's Sirat Rasul Allah. Oxford: Oxford UP, 1978.

Hohmann, Lew. Friedrich Wolf. Bilder einer deutschen Biographie. Berlin: Das europäische Buch, 1988.

Jehser, Werner. Friedrich Wolf. Sein Leben und Werk. Berlin: Volk und Wissen, 1968.

Müller, Henning. Friedrich Wolf: Weltbürger aus Neuwied. Neuwied: Peter Kehrein, 1988.

——. "Der jüdische Arzt und Kommunist Dr. Friedrich Wolf": Dokumente des Terrors und der Verfolgung 1931–1944. Neuwied: Stadtverwaltung Neuwied, 1988.

——. Wer war Wolf?. Cologne: Pahl-Rugenstein, 1988.

Pollatschek, Walther. Friedrich Wolf. Leben und Schaffen. Leipzig: Philipp Reclam, 1974.

Rodenberg, Hans. "Der Weg Friedrich Wolfs." Auf wieviel Pferden ich geritten . . . Der junge Friedrich Wolf: Eine Dokumentation. Ed. Emmi Wolf and Brigitte Struzyk. Berlin: Aufbau, 1988.

Schnabel, Manfred, Ed. Autorenporträt: Friedrich Wolf zum 100. Geburtstag. Berlin: Zentralinstitut für Bibliothekswesen, 1988.

Solbrig, Ingeborg. "Friedrich Wolf." Critical Survey of Drama: Foreign Language Series. Vol. 6. Pasadena: Salem, 1986. 2013–25.

Wolf, Emmi. "Der frühe Wolf. Friedrich Wolfs weltanschaulisch-philosophische Entwicklung 1888–1914." "Mut, nochmals Mut, immerzu Mut!": Protokollband "Internationales Wissenschaftliches Friedrich-Wolf-Symposium". Ed. Volkshochschule der Stadt Neuwied und Friedrich-Wolf-Archiv Lehnitz. Neuwied: Peter Kehrein, 1989/90.

Franz Werfel

Abels, Norbert. *Franz Werfel mit Selbstzeugnissen und Bilddokumenten.* Reinbek bei Hamburg: Rowohlt, 1990.

Buck, George C. "The Non-Creative Prose of Franz Werfel." *Franz Werfel: 1890–1945.* Ed. Lore B. Foltin. Pittsburgh: U Pittsburgh P, 1961.

Davidheiser, James C. "The Quest for Cultural and National Identity in the Works of Franz Werfel." *Perspectives on Contemporary Literature* 2 (1982): 58–66.

Foltin, Lore B. *Franz Werfel.* Stuttgart: Sammlung Metzler, 1972.

Grimm, Gunter E. "Ein hartnäckiger Wanderer. Zur Rolle des Judentums im Werk Franz Werfels." In *Im Zeichen Hiobs: Jüdische Schriftsteller und deutsche Literatur im 20. Jahrhundert.* Ed. Gunter Grimm, Hans-Peter Bayerdorfer, and Konrad Kwiet. Königstein/Ts.: Athenäum, 1985.

Jungk, Peter Stephan. *Franz Werfel: A Life in Prague, Vienna, and Hollywood.* New York: Grove Weidenfeld, 1990.

Kayser, Rudolf. "Franz Werfel." *Juden in der deutschen Literatur: Essays über zeitgenössische Schriftsteller.* Ed. Gustav Krojanker. Berlin: Welt-Verlag, 1922.

Lee, Maria Berl. "Agony, Pathos, and the Turkish Side in Werfel's *Die vierzig Tage des Musa Dagh.*" *West Virginia University Philological Papers* 31 (1986): 58–64.

Metzler, Oskar. "Franz Werfel." *Österreichische Literatur des 20. Jahrhunderts.* Ed. Horst Haase and Antal Madl. Berlin: Volk und Wissen, 1988.

Steiman, Lionel B. *Franz Werfel— The Faith of an Exile: From Prague to Beverly Hills.* Waterloo, Canada: Wilfrid Laurier UP, 1985.

Turrian, Marysia. *Dostojewskij und Franz Werfel: Vom östlichen zum westlichen Denken.* Bern: Paul Haupt, 1950.

Index